The

Handwork Teacher's Companion

A Curriculum Guide for Waldorf-Inspired Handwork Classes

Lili Blalock

The Handwork Teacher's Companion

Published by
Lili Koi Publishing
1161 Sylvan Place
Monterey, CA 93940
Liliblalock.com

Acknowledgements

I would like to acknowledge and thank the teachers and staff at the Rudolf Steiner College in Fairoaks, Ca. The Handwork Teacher Training Course has helped me both be a better teacher and gave me the information to write this book. A special thanks to Alecia Dodge for being such a thoughtful and supportive teacher and to Patricia Dickson for supporting the Subject Teacher Training Program.

Library of Congress Control Number: 2014916835

ISBN-13: 978-0-9908260-0-2

ISBN-10: 0-9908260-0-2

Manufactured in the United States of America

This book is dedicated to my children, Jeremy and Jesse, whose classes needed a handwork teacher and to my husband, Steve, who has tirelessly edited and problem solved to make an idea into a reality.

Table of Contents

By teaching the fingers and hands to be nimble and agile with a variety of processes and materials, students become confident in their ability to create their world. Work with the hands from 6 years old to fourteen sets the stage for clear thinking in later years. Passageways in the brain are created and kept open by the use of our hands. Without hands-on education, our society runs into the danger of becoming finger-blind, or losing the intelligence gained by working with our hands. By doing handwork, students are empowered to be able to work with their hands. By working with their hands, students come into an understanding of the unity in the material world.

Inner Preparation

There are a few things that I do every day to help in my teaching.

1) I prepare the room for the first class of the next day before I leave. For example if the first class of the day is first grade: I will move the chairs into a circle; put the work and nametags on the appropriate chairs; and put any supplies needed, say stuffing, yarn, needles and scissors into the middle of the circle. That way when I walk into the room, I am ready to go. I will also change the black boards for the next day's lessons. Along the same lines, I will mentally go over any unusual processes that will be happening the next day, such as dying or felting and gather the materials before I leave. If I am teaching in a class teacher's room, I will prepare the Handwork cart before I leave each day. I will make sure that all trash has been thrown out; needles, pins, threads and scissors are restocked and ready. I clean out and sort the yarn baskets each day after class also.

2) Each morning after I wake up, I write up a lesson plan for the day. For instance: first grade, knit, Baby buntings and rainbow balls; second grade, knit and crochet, Flute cases and gnomes; seventh grade, doll arms; fourth grade, stitch and sew, handwork bags.

3) On the way to work, I go over each class one more time, but this time, I say the opening verse and song, go over the projects and materials needed, rehearse any spoken instructions for the class and, finally, say the closing verse.

1.) Organize everything.
   a) Mark all containers.
   b) Have all yarn in an orderly fashion.
   c) Write out the rosters.
   d) Make the seating arrangements.
2.) Send or email a letter of welcome and introduction to the parents and students.
   a) Welcome them to the class
   b) Introduce myself
   c) Give an overview of the year
   d) Explain the first project
3.) Introduce Classroom Rules
   a) Follow directions the first time they are given and thereafter
   b) Raise your hand and wait for permission to speak
   c) Stay in your seat unless you have permission to do otherwise
   d) Keep hands, feet, and objects to yourself

- When I have my own classroom, I greet every student at the door, shake their hand and give them instructions concerning where to sit and to get to work quietly.

-If I am teaching in a class teacher's classroom, I wait to be invited into the room. Then walk to the front of the room and shake hands with the class teacher. We exchange greetings and then I greet the class.

- For first, second and third grades, chairs are arranged in a circle. In the beginning of the year, each chair has a nametag and the student's work on it. By the end of the year, students know where their seats are and I leave off the nametags. There is a circular cloth in the center of the circle with the yarn basket, work basket, a basket of sandpaper, a basket of rags, a jar of Beeswax pieces, a tin of yarn needles, a bowl of buttons and a basket of stuffing, as needed

-For fourth through eighth grades, students sit at tables and have assigned seats. I have a seating chart posted. Seats are changed monthly.

-There is a basket of supplies at each table, such as needles, scissors and sewing thread. There is a list of contents inside the basket for reference at the end of class.

-When I have a handwork room, 4th -8th grade students have individual cubbies to hold their work. As they enter the classroom they retrieve their work from their cubbies, sit down and get to work quietly. After the handwork bags have been completed, students are allowed to take their handwork home as homework as long as it returns on class days.

-Sewing Machines are kept in a cabinet and numbered to match the cubby numbers.

-After everyone has entered the classroom, we stand together silently with arms crossed on our chests, I say "Good Morning" or "Good Afternoon, _____ Grade". If there are any helpers, we greet them. We say our verse, sing our song and sit down quietly.

-I ask for quiet work for the first 10 minutes of class.

- Sometimes students like to have a challenge of working silently. Those who can work silently receive a sticker of appreciation.

-Students begin working on their projects.

-Beginning in fifth grade, project directions are written on a blackboard. Students check the blackboard for their class and write down new information from the board. When I go to their classroom, I bring a rolling chalkboard. Directions are written on the chalkboard and in several copies of my grade level book. Students are expected to write down the directions for the projects. Each step is demonstrated as we come to it. Collaboration with fellow students is encouraged.

-In 5th through 8th grades, I give a demonstration of the current step of the project we are working on.

-As the students work, I look around the circle and mark absences in the attendance book. On a separate line, I keep a record of each student's progress.

-Either the teacher or the helpers help the first graders to cast on and cast off. Second graders cast on and off for themselves. If they forget how to do it, I will demonstrate but allow them to do the work.

-I ask that they raise their hands if they need help. I call them one by one to come up to my chair. Alternatively, I go to them. Students are encouraged to help each other.

-For sewing classes, an ironing board is set up at the front of the classroom and as students need help, I either go to their seat or have them come up to the ironing board.

-Cross-stitch yarn and embroidery thread are cut to 36" lengths. They are tied onto stands with a lark's head knot. Students raise their hand with thumb and forefinger touching if they need thread or yarn. I can then silently nod to give them permission to get up and get what they need.

-After the ten minutes of quiet, students are allowed to speak softly with their neighbors for 5 minutes. Then we alternate between silence and soft visiting throughout the class.

-Students are allowed to use the restroom after the first 10 minutes of class.

- For first through fourth grades I give any directions, such as rows needed or casting on or off, verbally. Memorizing the patterns gives the teacher greater authority.

-If students ask me to fix a hole, I ask them if it is okay to pull out any stitches if necessary. I frequently ask students to count how many stitches are on their needles.

- For first, second and third grades, I go through their work after each class and correct mistakes.

- For first through fourth grades, when it is 5 minutes before the end of class, I sing the "Handwork time is over" song a couple of times and begin to put materials away. One child is assigned to collect the work that will stay in the handwork room. For students with nametags, I collect the nametags and put them in order as I collect them.

-For fifth through 8th grade, when it is 5 minutes before the end of class, I ring a bell and begin to put materials away. Students either return their work to their cubbies or their work in their handwork bags.

-For grades one, two, three and five, students are asked to wind up their yarn balls and stick their needles or hooks through the edges of the ball. Students are asked to rewind messy or unruly yarn balls.

-For grades four, six, seven and eight, the projects are folded neatly and placed either in a pile (for handwork bags in progress, doll bodies or other sewing projects) or put into handwork bags. All needles are to be turned in or stowed properly in and out of the fabric.

-I begin "Slap, clap, snap" -Slap your legs with your hands, clap hands together, snap fingers; repeat. Then begin the "My mother said" verse.

- We say our closing verse. I say, "Good-bye, _____ Grade" The students say goodbye. If there are any helpers, we say good-bye to them.

-For first grade, I ask one student to lead and one to be the caboose as students line up at the door to wait for their teacher

-When students have just learned to knit, I go through their work after each class and correct mistakes. After they have gotten the hang of it, I allow them to come to me if they see mistakes. If I notice an irregularity in the knitting, I will ask the student to look at the work with me and help them get back on track.

-Students are allowed to take their knitting to their classroom if it is okay with their class teacher. In grades one through three, handwork is not to go home. If the yarn comes back in a snarl, students must help in rerolling the yarn ball and are given one more chance to keep their work tidy. If the work comes back in a mess, they must leave their work in class. Some class teachers require the students to bring a bag to carry their work. Some class teachers have a parent make bags for the class. Some class teachers carry the work back and forth to class in a basket. Some class teachers do not allow their students to bring their work to class.

-Students are encouraged to come to me during recess or after school if they need help.

Classroom Needs:
  Baskets for holding work
  Cubbies for holding work for 4th -8th grades, if available
  Scissors:
    Yarn and thread scissors
    Paper scissors
    Fabric Scissors
  Blocks to hold scissors
  Size H Crochet hook for fixing work
  Needles:
    Yarn Needles #13
    Tapestry needles size 16 and 22
    Gold Eye Embroidery Needles
    Chenille Needles
    Doll Needles
  Containers for needles and/or Needle Books
  Sewing Thread in white, black and colors to match project fabrics
  Wooden racks for holding Perle cotton and cross stitch yarn
  Materials to make knitting needles:
    100 grit sand paper
    220 grit sand paper
    Basket for sandpaper
    Beeswax cut into small pieces
    Rags for buffing
  Book for keeping track of attendance and individual progress
  For Hand Felting:
    Tubs for holding water for felting
    Drying tray, ground cover/bedding plant tray
    Hand Soap
  Hand Cards or dog brushes in pairs
  Graphite Pencil for each student
  Iron
  Ironing Board
  Yellow Pencil
  Pins
  Pincushion
  Crochet hook, size H, for fixing dropped stitches
  Basket to hold yarn
  Basket to hold Fleece for stuffing
  Sewing Needles for sewing buttons on
  Thread
  Buttons
  Tailor's Chalk
  Pins

Pincushion
Roller Cutter for the teacher's use
Roller Cutter Pad
Sewing Machines/ one per each student (ideal)
Seam Rippers
Tape Measures
Graphite Pencil for each student
Baskets of various sizes to hold fabric
Large Plastic Tubs to store fabric
Chalk
Chalkboard
Eraser

1ˢᵗ Grade Verses

Opening Verse

My hands are a bowl
They hold water just fine
My hands are a shelter,
A pillow, a line.
My hands hold the nail

And the hammer, too.
My hands are my most useful tools.

Song

We use our hands to fashion,
The feelings of our hearts.
We thank this beautiful planet,
And all the stars above.
We now ask for a blessing,
From planet Earth and sky,
That we may do our handwork
With our hearts and hands and minds.

Slap, Clap, Snap:

My mother said
I never should
Play with the fairies
In the wood
They dance with fire
They roll in hay
They'll steal your heart
right away.

Closing Verse

Handwork time is over
Our work for now is done.
Our busy hands have served us well,
Now head, heart, hands are one.

Extra Verse

Yo ho ho, Josie finished a row!

Lesson Plan for Handwork

Grade one:

THE GOALS FOR THIS YEAR ARE:

- To set the stage for all the handwork classes to follow
- To form good habits in taking care of work and materials
- To foster an appreciation for natural materials
- To begin to develop a sense of color
- To learn to be self-sufficient and feel that "I can do"
- To become aware of the quality of their work

THE MAIN SKILLS TO BE INTRODUCED AND FURTHER DEVELOPED THIS YEAR ARE:

- To learn and become proficient at finger knitting
- To sand and finish a pair of wooden knitting needles
- To learn to knit
- To learn to sew in ends in a knitting project
- To learn to tie a simple knot
- To learn to wet felt
- To learn to shape their knitting with "knit 2 together"

TIME LINE OF PROJECTS: (Class is held 2 times a week for 50 minutes each)

August-September
- Finger knitted cord for nametag
- Jump rope

October-December
- Sand and finish knitting needles with beeswax
- Baby bunting
- Folded paper star

January-June
- Rainbow ball
- Kitty
- Scarf
- Lamb
- Lion
- Duck
- Bag
- Elephant
- Felted Egg

The children entering first grade are entering the second seven-year phase of their childhood and are ready to learn. They have a deep felt need to be taken seriously and are ready to begin work. They are still seamlessly connected with the world and so we work with the continuous thread, always staying connected to the whole. The first project is a finger knitted nametag. Most of the children have finger knitted in Kindergarten and joyfully dive into the project. After that the children make a jump rope from a finger knitted strand. The students smooth dowels with sandpaper and beeswax to make their knitting needles. Knitting is introduced with a story and the knitting begins. Early projects are rectangles or squares that are sewn into different shapes, such as baby buntings, cats and balls.

The first project I start with in first grade is finger knitting, also known as finger crocheting. Some children know how to finger knit and for some it is new. The first project is a string for their nametags. I make nametags for first graders because they are all new at once. The nametags are strips of painted watercolor paper with the student's name and class number written on it. Class numbers are obtained by putting the students' first names in alphabetical order and numbering from 1-24.

How to finger Knit:

With yarn, make a slipknot. Hold onto the knot with the left hand, with the right hand reach through the loop of the slipknot and grab the yarn. Pull up a new loop through the old loop. Keep pulling until the first loop is tight. Adjust the new loop size by pulling on the tail of the yarn. Repeat until the finger knitting is long enough for use or until you get tired or run out of yarn.

Here are 2 verses for finger knitting or make up your own:

> *Reach in the hole and catch the worm.*
>
> Or: *Catch the gopher, close up the hole.*

Name Tag String

6 yard ball of worsted weight wool or cotton yarn in one color, for example blue

Finger knit the entire ball. Tie the ends into holes punched into the sides of the nametag.

Jump Rope

Brown Sheep Burly Spun Yarn- 30 yard ball
Finger knit the entire ball of yarn.
Re-finger knit the finger knitted strand
The first finger knitting seems to take forever! But, the re-finger knitting goes surprisingly quickly and is often finished in one class!
Try it out. Too long? Tie the ends into loops.

¼" diameter hardwood dowels, cut to 9" lengths, 2/student
100-grit sandpaper
220-grit sandpaper
Beeswax
Rag for buffing
2 beads with 1/4" hole to fit dowels
White glue
Sharpie marker

Write the student's name one inch from one end of each dowel. Sand the other end of each dowel into a tapered point with the 100-grit sandpaper. Support the dowel with your index finger while sanding. Make sure the point is long and gradually tapers to a gentle point, like a long tall gnome hat.

Sand the entire needle with the 220-sandpaper until it is as smooth as silk.

Coat the sanded needle all over with beeswax.

Use the rag to buff the needle until it is smooth.

Glue one bead onto the end of each dowel. Let dry before using.

Wool to Yarn Puppet Show

It is fun to show the process of turning raw wool into a finished product with a puppet show.

Props
Main character Doll
Lamb
Raw sheep's wool
Clean Sheep's Wool
A small pot
Scissors
Drying tray or rack
Hand Cards
Spindle
Flowers
Yellow yarn
Knitting needles
A Yellow Hat to fit the Main Character

The Lamb Said "Baaa"

"Baaaaaa"

Jolie started from her sleep. That sounded like a lamb and it sounded really close. Jolie's family raised sheep, so she was used to the sound of sheep and lambs. But the sheep lived outside in the fields and in the barn. The "baa" she had heard sounded much closer.

"Baaaaa"

There it was again! That was very close! Was it coming from the kitchen? Jolie jumped out of bed and ran downstairs.

"Baaaaa"

The sound was louder in the kitchen. Over in the corner behind the stove Jolie could just see the top of a fuzzy head over the side of a box.

"There's a lamb in the kitchen!" she exclaimed

A ewe had given birth to the lamb in the night but couldn't take care of it. Jolie petted the lamb. It was so soft. The lamb reached up to nibble Jolie's fingers.

Her father handed her a bottle of milk. The lamb sucked eagerly on the milk. It drank and drank.

From that day on Jolie took care of the lamb and the lamb took care of Jolie.

One day, it was time for the lamb to have a haircut. *(Cover the lamb puppet in a layer of raw sheep's wool; pretend to cut it off either with scissors or two fingers.)*

"I wish I could keep it with me always" Jolie said.

Jolie walked over to her neighbor Mrs. Willis's house with her bag of wool.

Mrs. Willis said she would be happy to help Jolie with her wool.

"First we will wash the wool," she said to Jolie. (*Have a pot with clean wool locks inside, put the raw wool locks just "sheared" off the lamb into the pot, swish the pot around for a few seconds. Then pull out the clean wool locks.*)

They laid the fleece out to dry. (*Lay the clean locks on a drying tray or rack*)

Mrs. Willis showed Jolie how to gently open the locks and card the wool on hand cards. (*Open the locks and load them onto a hand card. Card the fleece and roll it into a rolag*)

Mrs. Willis handed a drop spindle to Jolie. The spindle twirled as the fleece twisted into yarn. (*Spin the rolag on a drop spindle*)

Jolie gathered flowers for dye. Jolie carefully put the flower clippings into the pot and watched it boil. (*Put some flowers into the pot*)

Mrs. Willis helped Jolie wind her yarn into skeins. (*Wrap the yarn from the drop spindle around your hand and tie*)

Jolie carefully put the yarn into the dye pot. (*Put the skein into the dye pot*)

When they pulled the yarn out it had turned a sunny yellow. (*Pull out a small skein of yellow yarn*)

The yarn was hung to dry.

Mrs. Willis showed Jolie how to knit the lamb's fleece! (*Pull out knitting needles with yellow yarn cast on and knit a row*)

Jolie put on her new hat. (*Have a small yellow hat that fits the puppet or doll or a human size.*)

Jolie showed the lamb her new hat and the lamb said, "baa"!

The Story of the Knitting Verse

"Under the root,
Around the Dome,
Catch a Tomten,
And bring him home."

Once upon a time not too long ago near a forest not too far from here, there lived a Tomten in a cozy space underneath the floorboards of a barn. The Tomten lived with his wife and his children. He had so many children, that he wasn't quite sure how many children he had. They wore warm woolen clothing that they made themselves by gathering the sheep's wool that caught on the fences and knitting it into sweaters, and socks and caps and gloves. The Tomten children were very good and helped their mother around the house and cleaned up after themselves except that they had one very bad habit, they liked to tease the animals of the forest.

Every night all the Tomtens would gather at their long table, they had benches to sit on because there were a lot of children, no one knew quite how many. Mother Tomten would bring a big pot of steaming porridge to the table and scoop a steaming serving into each bowl. Before she passed it onto the children, she would place a large pat of golden butter into the middle of the porridge. And as it was passed from tomten to tomten, the butter would melt into a golden pool. The tomtens loved their porridge and so they had it every night. You could count on the tomten children to leave whatever they were doing in the forest to show up for the porridge.

The Tomtens lived in a barn right next to the forest and many animals lived in the forest. In the very middle of the forest, under a tall, tall tree there lived a fox. He had dug himself a cozy den under the roots of the tree. The fox loved the animals of the forest. Best of all, he loved chickens. He could eat chickens anytime! One day, the fox was napping in his cozy den, dreaming wonderful dreams about chasing rabbits and his other forest friends; when he was awaken from his dreams by the sounds of clucking. He sat up and looked about, shook his head and wondered, "was that a chicken?" Then he slowly crept out of his den over the big round rock, and under the root.

He looked to the left,
He looked to the right,
But there was not a chicken in sight.

The fox scratched his head and thought, "that was strange." He walked back to his den and went under the root, and over the big, round, domed rock, curled up and went back to sleep.

A few days later the fox was napping in his den having wonderful dreams about squirrels. When what should wake him from his dreams but the sound of clucking chickens. "Chickens in my forest?" thought the fox. Then he slowly crept out of his den over the big, round rock, and under the root.

He looked to the left,
He looked to the right,
But there was not a chicken in sight.

"This is very strange," thought the fox.   He walked back to his den and went under the root, and over the big, round, domed rock, curled up and went back to sleep.

Well, a couple of days later, the fox had just settled down for a nice sleep and thoughts about quail, when what should startle him out of his reveries? Chickens? Clucking chickens? Again? Well, he was not going to miss them this time! The fox scrambled over the rock and accidently tripped over the root and landed nose over teakettle flat on his back on the forest floor. He opened his eyes and

> *He looked to the left,*
> *He looked to the right,*
> *But there was not a chicken in sight.*

But what was that? A giggle? Coming from the tall, tall tree in the center of the forest? His own tall, tall tree? He looked up squinting into the sunlight and what should he see sitting on the branches but Tomtens, lots of tomtens, so many tomtens, he was not quite sure how many. And they were laughing at him! Why, there had never been any chickens at all. It was the Tomten children playing a trick on him! The fox got up off the ground and thought to himself, "I'm going to teach those Tomten children a thing or two about playing a trick on a fox!"

One day not too much later, mother Tomten stood at the long, long table about to serve the nightly porridge as it steamed fragrantly in the pot. She glanced along one side of the table and then glanced at the other side. It seemed that there were fewer children at the table. She paused in her serving and said to Father Tomten, "Does it look like there are fewer children, dear?"

He laughed, "Oh, you know our little tomtens, how they get involved in their games and explorations. They'll come home. Don't you worry."

So Mother Tomten scooped the steaming porridge into bowls and placed a large pat of golden butter right in the middle of each serving before she passed it along the table.

A few days later, mother Tomten stood at the long, long table about to serve the nightly porridge as it steamed fragrantly in the pot. She glanced along one side of the table and then glanced at the other side. It seemed that there were fewer and fewer children at the table. She paused in her serving and said to Father Tomten, "Does it look like there are even fewer children?"

He laughed, "Oh, you know our little tomtens, how they get involved in their games and explorations. They'll come home. Don't you worry."

So Mother Tomten scooped the steaming porridge into bowls and placed a large pat of golden butter right in the middle of each serving before she passed it along the table.

Well, A few days later, mother Tomten stood at the long, long table about to serve the nightly porridge as it steamed fragrantly in the pot. She glanced along one side of the table and then glanced at the other side. There was not a single Tomten child at the table! Mother Tomten looked at Father Tomten down the long empty table, and Father Tomten said, "Let's go find our children!"

The tomtens looked in the caves and under the fallen trees, they wandered the farm and the forest calling out to their lost children. They found not a trace nor heard a peep. They searched all of the children's' favorite hiding places but no children. Eventually Father Tomten found himself in the middle of the forest next to the tall, tall tree. Father Tomten remembered that there was a fox's den under the tall, tall tree. He called down into the den and lo and behold he heard a faint cry back. He reached his arm down into the den but it was too deep. Father Tomten searched around for a stick to reach down into the den but all he could find was a short branch. Just about that time, Mother tomten came walking past.

"I've found our children," cried Father Tomten joyously. "I just can't get them out."

Mother Tomten squealed with delight that the children were found and then set about to get them out. "I just saw a fallen tree a little ways back!" she exclaimed.

The tomtens walked back to the tree but it was so heavy they could not lift it. Just then three woodcutters came walking through the forest.

"Oh," cried the tomtens to the woodcutters. "Would you please help us carry this tree to the fox's den so that we can free our children?"

The woodcutters gladly helped them. All five of them walked back to the den carrying the tree. Then they reached

"Under the root,
Around the Dome,
Catch a Tomten,
And bring him home."

Out popped a tomten child! Again they reached

"Under the root,
Around the Dome,
Catch a Tomten,
And bring him home."

And again and again they reached into the den:

"Under the root,
Around the Dome,
Catch a Tomten,
And bring him home."

Until every tomten child was freed from the fox's den! The tomtens were all so happy that every body was hugging everybody else. Finally when the last tomten was freed, they thanked the woodcutters for their help and walked back to their cozy home under the floorboards of the barn. Mother tomten cooked up a big pot of porridge and made sure that each bowl had an extra large pat of golden butter melted on top. All the tomten children had a much-needed bath and every one went to bed without a complaint! Father tomten told them all a story about being kind to the animals of the forest and they all went to sleep.

And do you know what else happened? The fox learned something too!
(Show the fox puppet with knitting needles, saying:

"Under the root,
Around the Dome,
Catch a Tomten,
And bring him home.")

In telling the tomten story, it is good to have some characters that you have made to add interest to the story. I have a hand knitted fox puppet and a little tomten doll with a tall red hat. The tomten starts out the story, just kind of being on my lap. When the fox is introduced, the fox puppet acts out the story, looking for chickens, falling over, etc. When the parents find the tomten children in the fox's den, I pull out a knitting needle and use that to motion, "Under the root, around the dome, catch a tomten and bring him home." Finally, at the end of the story, I bring the fox back holding small knitting needles and saying under his breath, "Under the root..."

Materials:
Brown Sheep Lamb's Pride Worsted Weight: Blue
Knitting Needles size 8
Darning Needle

Cast on 20 stitches. Knit until the piece is as long as the knitting needles or about 9".

Bind off leaving a 12" tail.

Thread the yarn from the bind off edge into the darning needle, fold the bind off edge in half and sew across. Sew yarn end inside.

Fold the cast on edge up to form a pouch, about 2/3's of the length. Thread darning needle with blue yarn and attach the yarn at a corner of the cast on edge. Sew the side with whipstitch; sew in yarn ends. Repeat for other side of the pouch.

Finger knit a chain about 18" long (as long as a desk top.) Thread the finger knitting onto a darning needle, starting at the center front of the cast on edge, sew the finger knitting in and out around the baby bunting, skipping several knit stitches at a time.

Place the baby into the bunting and tie a bow to hold the baby in.

Baby:

Materials: 9" square cotton stockinette in skin color
 Thread in matching color
 Sewing needle
Wool fleece for stuffing
 Mohair yarn for hair
Crochet hook size I

To make baby: Fold stockinette into quarters, mark the center. Open the stockinette out and draw a 3"diameter circle with a pencil and compass. Baste around the circle; do not knot the thread. Wind a small ball of fleece roving, about the size of a golf ball and place on the center of the stockinette, pull up the basting threads tightly to make the neck and tie or sew a knot. Smooth out any wrinkles. Crochet a small cap from the yarn and sew onto the head.

Hair cap: chain 6, slip stitch in the first chain to a form ring.
Row 1: work 6 single crochets into the center of the ring
Row 2: work 2 single crochets into each single crochet of the previous row.
 Row 3: work 1 single crochet into each single crochet of the previous row.
Try the cap on the doll. Is it the right size or does it need another round? When complete, fasten the yarn off.

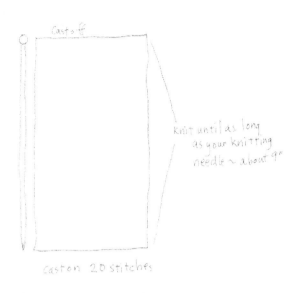

Cast off

Knit until as long
as your knitting
needle ~ about 9"

cast on 20 stitches

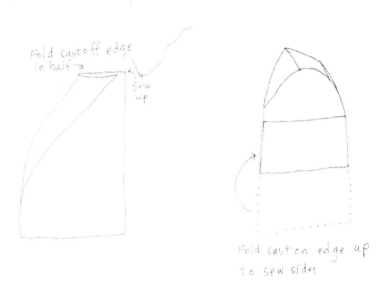

Fold cast off edge
in half

Sew
up

Fold cast on edge up
to sew sides

Baby Bunting Assembly

Red, orange, yellow, green, blue, purple
-Sung to "Twinkle, twinkle little star."

Rainbow Ball

Brown Sheep Lamb's Pride Worsted weight yarn, a one-ounce ball of each in: Red, Orange, Yellow, Green, Blue and Purple
Knitting Needles-size 8
Yarn Needle size 13
Fleece for stuffing

With red, cast on 20 stitches, knit 14 rows-7 garter stitch ridges on each side. Cut the red yarn and tie on the orange yarn.

Knit 14 rows with the orange yarn-7 garter stitch ridges on each side. Cut the orange yarn and tie on the yellow yarn.

Knit 14 rows with the yellow yarn-7 garter stitch ridges on each side. Cut the yellow yarn and tie on the green yarn.

Knit 14 rows with the green yarn-7 garter stitch ridges on each side. Cut the green yarn and tie on the blue yarn.

Knit 14 rows with the blue yarn -7 garter stitch ridges on each side. Cut the blue yarn and tie on the purple yarn.

Knit 14 rows with the purple yarn-7 garter stitch ridges on each side. Bind off leaving an 18-inch tail for sewing up.

With the yarn left at the bind off edge and the yarn needle, sew the cast on edge to the bind off edge using a whipstitch. Knot the yarn.

Sew a running stitch around one open edge and pull tightly to gather the knitting. Take a few stitches across from one color to another to pull the edges together.

Stuff with fleece. Sew a running stitch around the open edge and pull tightly to gather together. Take a few stitches across from one color to another to pull the end together. Knot firmly and sew tail to inside.

Rainbow Ball

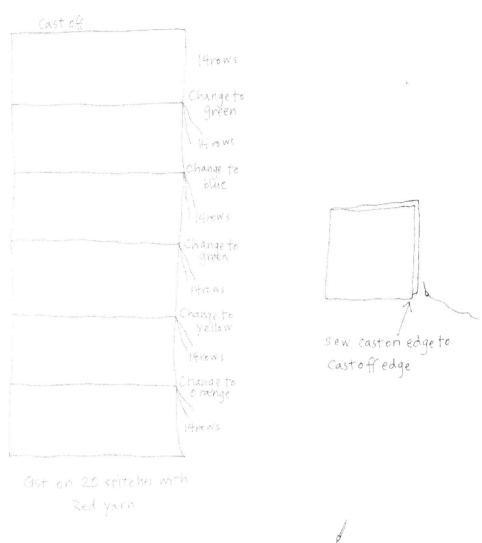

Cast off

14rows

Change to green

14 rows

Change to blue

14rows

Change to green

14rows

Change to yellow

14rows

Change to orange

14rows

Cast on 20 stitches with
Red yarn

Sew cast on edge to
Cast off edge

running stitch

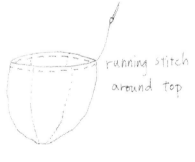

running stitch
around top

Brown Sheep Lamb's Pride Worsted weight yarn
Knitting Needles-size 8
Yarn Needle size 13
Fleece for stuffing

Body:

Cast on 20 stitches. Knit until you almost have a square about 40 rows. Bind off

Head:

Cast on 9 stitches. Knit until the piece matches the body length. Bind off

Tail:

Cast on 3 stitches. Knit until the piece matches the body length. Bind off

Sewing up

Body:

Fold each corner diagonally into a leg and sew up about half way across the side with a yarn needle. Repeat for each leg. Leave the tummy open for stuffing. Stuff firmly with fleece and sew up.

Head:

 Fold in half lengthwise into a square and sew up 2 sides. Stuff firmly with fleece and sew up. Form ears by taking a stitch in the center of one side from the edge to the middle. Pull firmly. Repeat several times. Attach to one end of the body with several stitches.

Tail:

Fold in half lengthwise and sew up. Attach to opposite end of the body from the head.

Sew all ends in.

Kitty

Body:
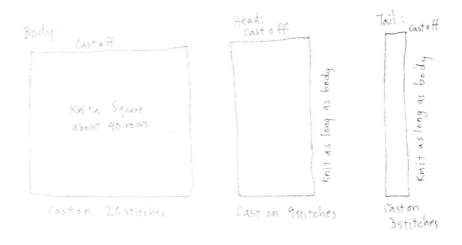
Cast off

Knit a Square
about 48 rows

Cast on 20 stitches

Head:
Cast off

Knit as long as body

Cast on 9 stitches

Tail:
Cast off

Knit as long as body

Cast on 3 stitches

Find a square
Fold corner up

when lower edge/corner crosses to top corner to form a triangle = square

Legs
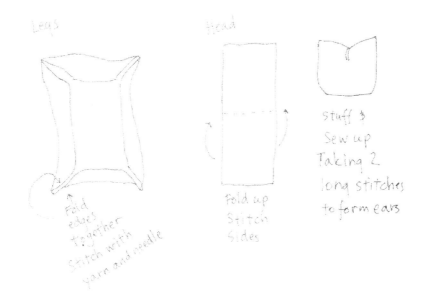
Fold edges together stitch with yarn and needle

Head
Fold up Stitch Sides

stuff &
Sew up
Taking 2
long stitches
to form ears

33

Kitty 2

Legs:

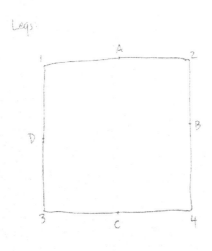

Leg 1 = Fold A to D; sew edge from
AD to 1

Leg 2 = Fold A to B; sew edge from
AB to point 2

Leg 3 - Fold C to D; sew edge from
CD to 3

Leg 4 - Fold C to B; sew edge from
CB to point 4

Knitting Worsted
Size 8 Needles
Yarn Needle #13
Crochet hook size H, for fringe

1) Cast on 20 stitches.
2) Knit until the scarf reaches a student's toes when the project is held up to the student's nose.
3) Bind off. Sew in ends.
4) If desired add fringe: Cut yarn pieces 8" long. Fold in half and pull a loop through the cast off edge with the crochet hook. Pull the ends of the yarn through the loop and pull to tighten. Continue across the bind off edge. Repeat across the Cast on edge.

At first I allowed students to change colors as they saw fit but soon realized that the enthusiasm for colors led to yarn changes every row and many, many fringed tails hanging. These were not as enthusiastically sewn in. So now I require at least 20 rows of each color before a color change. This creates many fewer ends to sew in. I also ask the student to sew in the yarn ends of the last color before I allow them to move onto the next color.

White knitting worsted
Knitting needles size 8
Yarn Needle
Wool Fleece for stuffing

Back Legs:
Cast on 36 stitches. Knit 16 rows. At the beginning of the next row, bind off 8 stitches; knit to the end of the row. At the beginning of the next row, bind off 8 stitches; knit to the end of the row.

Tummy:
Knit 12 rows.
Front legs:
Cast on 8 stitches at the end of each of the next two rows, 36 stitches total. Knit 14 more rows, 16 rows total.

Head:
At the beginning of the next row, bind off 12 stitches; knit to the end of the row. At the beginning of the next row, bind off 12 stitches; knit to the end of the row. Knit 24 rows. Bind off.

To sew up:
Fold one back leg in half, sew across hoof and up leg to tummy. Repeat for the other back leg. Stuff firmly. Fleece can be wrapped around a slender object, such as a pencil or scissors, to form a cylinder and then slid into position in the leg while the stuffing is still on the core. Sew up the front legs and stuff in a similar manner. Sew a running stitch along the rump and pull tightly to gather. Sew between the back legs, up the tummy and between the front legs making sure that the legs align with each other. Stuff the tummy. Fold the head along the short edge and sew up along the bind off edge. Fold head in half, back towards the body and sew along one side edge. Stuff and sew along the other side edge, leaving the chin open for stuffing. Stuff firmly and sew up under the chin. Finger knit a 2-3" chain for the tail and sew into a loop for the tail.

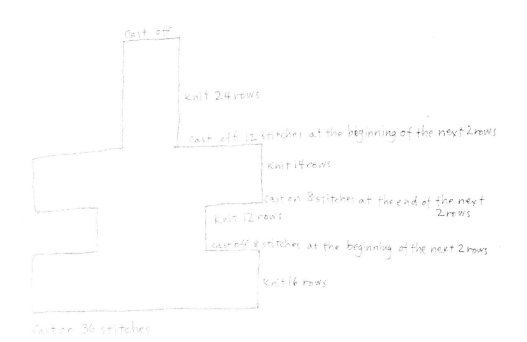

Cast off

Knit 24 rows

Cast off 12 stitches at the beginning of the next 2 rows

Knit 14 rows

Cast on 8 stitches at the end of the next 2 rows

Knit 12 rows

Cast off 8 stitches at the beginning of the next 2 rows

Knit 16 rows

Cast on 36 stitches

Fold legs in half & sew up

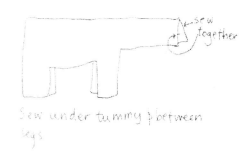

Sew together

Sew under tummy & between legs

Lion

Knitting worsted: Tawny gold yarn for the lion body
                   Brown yarn for the mane
Knitting needles size 8
Yarn needle #13
Crochet hook size H
Wool for stuffing

Back Legs

With gold yarn, cast on 40 stitches. Knit 20 rows. At the beginning of the next row, bind off 10 stitches, knit to the end of the row. At the beginning of the next row, bind off 10 stitches, knit to the end of the row.

Tummy

Knit 16 rows. Cast on 10 stitches at the end of each of the next two rows, 40 stitches total.

Front Legs

Knit 20 rows. At the beginning of the next row, bind off 8 stitches, knit to the end of the row. At the beginning of the next row, bind off 8 stitches, knit to the end of the row.

Head

Knit 24 rows. Cut yarn leaving a 12" tail. Thread yarn onto a yarn needle and run it through the stitches on the needle. Pull to gather stitches tightly together and knot the yarn. Sew the lower edge of head up to the front legs. Knot the yarn.

Sewing up

Fold one back leg in half; sew across the foot and up the leg to the tummy. Repeat for the other back leg. Stuff firmly. Fleece can be wrapped around a slender object, such as a pencil or scissors, to form a cylinder and then slid into position in the leg while still on the core. Sew up the front legs and stuff in a similar manner. Sew a running stitch along the rump and pull tightly to gather together. Sew between back legs, and half way up the tummy. Stuff the tummy. Sew from the tummy and between the front legs making sure that they align with each other. Fasten off the yarn. Sew in all yarn ends. Finger knit for 2-3" and sew on for the tail.

Ears

Finger knit 1" with gold yarn. Sew in place on top of the head for the ear. Repeat for the second ear.

Mane

Cut yarn into 4" lengths. Fold yarn in half and with a crochet hook pull up a loop around the lion's face, pull the yarn ends through the loop. Continue adding yarn loops around the face until the mane looks full.

Baby Bunting

Rainbow Ball

Kitty

Nose to Toes Scarf

Lamb

Lion

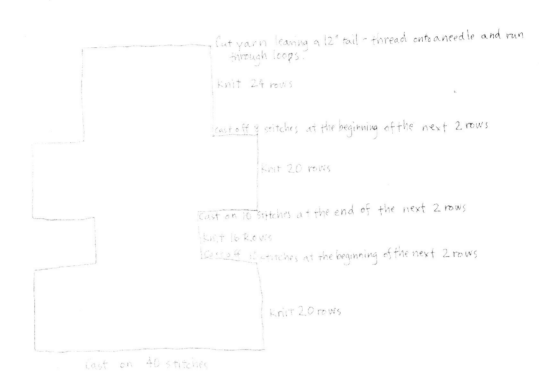

Cut yarn leaving a 12" tail - thread onto a needle and run through loops.

Knit 24 rows

Cast off 3 stitches at the beginning of the next 2 rows

Knit 20 rows

Cast on 10 stitches at the end of the next 2 rows

Knit 16 Rows

Cast off 10 stitches at the beginning of the next 2 rows

Knit 20 rows

Cast on 40 stitches

Sew up legs & stuff

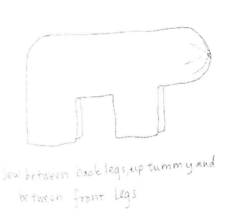

Sew between back legs up tummy and between front legs

White or brown knitting worsted
Orange yarn for bill
Dark yarn for eye
Knitting needles size 8
Yarn needle
Crochet hook size H
Wool for stuffing

Directions are for duckling; directions for the duck are in parentheses ()

Head:
Cast on 8 (12) stitches. Knit 12 (20) rows or enough to make a square.
At the end of the last row, cast on 7 (12) stitches, 15 (24) stitches total.

Body:
Knit 29 (45) rows, ending at the narrow end of the work
At the beginning of the next row, bind off 7 (12) stitches; knit to the end of the row.

Head:
Knit 12 (20) rows. Bind off.

Sewing up:
Fold the knitting in half length wise, matching up the heads. Sew up the short end of the body, across the back and up the back of the head. Sew the bind off and cast on edges of the head together; knot yarn. Sew a running stitch around the duck's neck; leave the yarn ends long. With the yarn needle and yarn, sew a running stitch around the front of the duck's head; pull tightly to gather and knot. Stuff the duck firmly; shape the tail by pulling up on the back seam. Sew a running stitch around the duck's breast and pull tightly to gather; knot yarn and sew in ends. Pull the running stitch around the duck's neck to shape the head and neck; knot yarn and sew in ends.

Because the first graders have not learned to crochet yet, I crochet the bill and sew on the eyes for the students.

Bill:
With the crochet hook and orange yarn, pull up a loop of yarn slightly to the side of where the bill should be on the duck's head; work 2 (3) single crochets into the duck's head to form the bill; chain 1; turn work.
Work 1 single crochet into each single crochet and chain in the previous row-3 single crochets; chain 1; turn work.
Decrease: Pull up a loop in the next 2 single crochets, 3 loops on the hook, pull the yarn through all 3 loops; work 1 single crochet; fasten off the yarn. Sew in the ends.

Eyes:

Mark the location of the eyes with sewing pins. With dark yarn, thread the yarn needle and coming through the duck's head, a little to the side of one pin, take a ¼" stitch. Take one more stitch in the same place, don't pull too tightly. Take the yarn across through the duck's head to the other eye and take 2 more stitches; sew through the duck's head and out the back. Trim yarn ends.

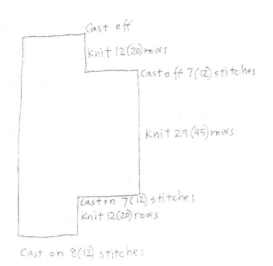

Cast off

Knit 12(20) rows

Cast off 7(12) stitches

Knit 29(45) rows

Cast on 7(12) stitches
Knit 12(20) rows

Cast on 8(12) stitches

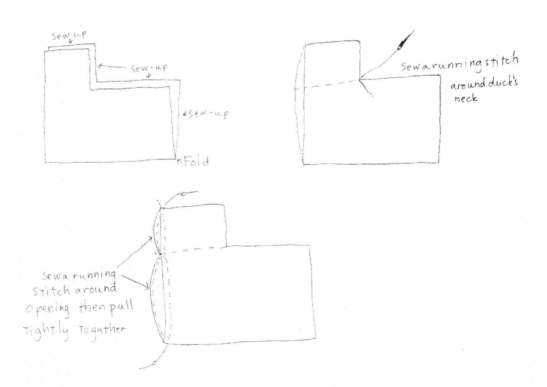

Sew up

Sew-up

Sew-up

Fold

Sew a running stitch around duck's neck

Sew a running stitch around opening then pull tightly together

Knitting worsted yarn in three or more colors
Knitting needles size 8
Yarn needle
Button
Thread and needle for sewing button on

Front:
Cast on 30 stitches.
Knit 60 rows; break yarn. Join new yarn color

Back:
Knit 60 rows; break yarn.
Join new yarn color

Flap:
Decrease row: Knit 2 together; knit to the end of the row.
Repeat the decrease row until only 1 stitch remains. Pull the loop off the needle and use it to begin finger knitting for 2", about 10 loops. Cut the yarn leaving a 12" tail. Sew in all the ends except the 12" tail.

Sewing up:
Fold the front of the bag over the back of the bag; the flap should extend past the front. With yarn and yarn needle, join the yarn to one side edge and sew the back and front together along the side using a whipstitch. Knot the yarn and sew in the ends. Sew up the other side in the same way.

Button:
Sew the 12"tail at the end of the flap back into the flap to form a loop with the finger knitting. Thread the needle with the thread, pull the ends together and knot. Fold the flap over the front of the bag and mark where the finger knitted loop lands with your finger. Pull the needle through the spot just marked. Catch the knot with the needle. Run the needle up and down through the holes in the button then catch the knitted fabric without going through to the opposite side of the bag. Repeat 3 more times. Knot the thread and trim the ends.

Strap:
Cast on 7 stitches and knit for 24". Bind off.
Sew the strap to the sides of the bag.

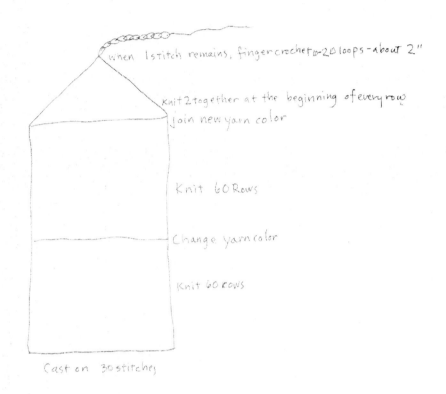

when 1 stitch remains, finger crochet ~20 loops - about 2"

Knit 2 together at the beginning of every row
Join new yarn color

Knit 60 Rows

Change yarn color

Knit 60 rows

Cast on 30 stitches

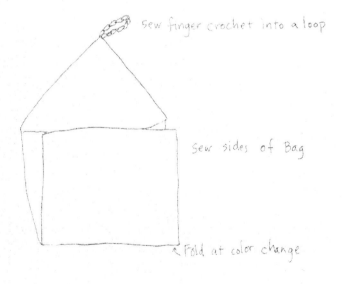

Sew finger crochet into a loop

Sew sides of Bag

Fold at color change

Grey knitting worsted yarn
Knitting needles size 8
Yarn Needle
Wool Fleece for stuffing

Back Legs:
Cast on 40 stitches. Knit 20 rows.
At the beginning of the next 2 rows, bind off 8 stitches; knit to the end of the row.

Tummy:
Knit 12 rows.
Cast on 8 stitches at the end of each of the next two rows, 40 stitches total.

Front legs:
Knit 18 rows.

Head:
At the beginning of the next 2 rows, bind off 10 stitches; knit to the end of the row.
Knit 16 rows.
Knit 2 stitches together, at the beginning of every row, 12 times.
Knit 20 rows. Bind off.

To sew up:
Fold one back leg in half; sew across the foot and up the leg to the tummy. Repeat for the other back leg. Stuff firmly. Fleece can be wrapped around a slender object as a core, such as a pencil or scissors, to form a cylinder and then slid into position in the leg while it is still on the core. Sew up the front legs and stuff in a similar manner. Sew a running stitch along the rump and pull tightly to gather. Sew between the back legs, up the tummy and between the front legs making sure that they align with each other. Stuff the tummy. Fold the head and trunk in half and sew up, adding stuffing every inch or so along the way. Sew a running stitch around the bind off seam of the trunk and pull tightly to gather. Knot the yarn and sew in the ends. Finger knit a 2-3" chain for the tail and sew in place.

Ears:
Cast on 10 stitches and knit until you have a square.
Repeat for the other ear.
Sew a running stitch around 3 sides of the square and pull gently to curve in.
Sew the flat edge of the ear onto the head vertically an inch behind the trunk.
Sew in all ends.

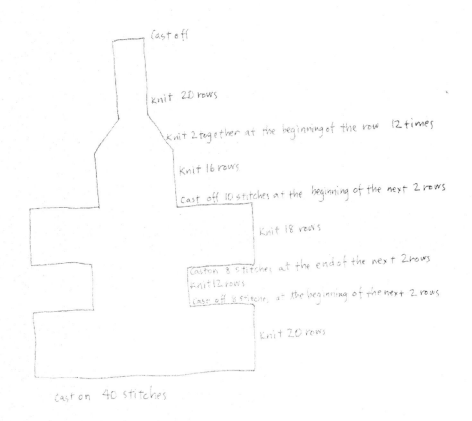

Cast off

Knit 20 rows

Knit 2 together at the beginning of the row   12 times

Knit 16 rows

Cast off 10 stitches at the beginning of the next 2 rows

Knit 18 rows

Cast on 8 stitches at the end of the next 2 rows
Knit 12 rows
Cast off 8 stitches at the beginning of the next 2 rows

Knit 20 rows

Cast on 40 stitches

46

Ducks

Bag

Elephant

Opening:
I look at my hands with fingers so fine
And I want to be proud that they are mine.
For deep in my heart lies a golden chest
With secret treasures that no one can guess.
Unless, my hands do their very best
To work and work and open that chest.

Purling:
Through the gate
Catch the goat
Back we go
Jump off the boat

Slap, Clap, Snap:
My mother said I never should
Play with the fairies in the wood
They dance with fire
They roll in hay
They'll steal your heart right away.

Closing:
Handwork time is over.
Our work for now is done.
Our busy hands have served us well.
Now head, heart and hands are one.

Lesson Plan for Handwork

Grade two:
THE GOALS FOR THIS YEAR ARE:

- To approach creating with joy
- To form good habits in taking care of work and materials
- To foster an appreciation for natural materials
- To begin to develop a sense for color
- To learn to be self-sufficient and feel that "I can do"
- To become aware of the quality of their work
- To begin thinking and designing in 3-dimensions

THE MAIN SKILLS TO BE INTRODUCED AND FURTHER DEVELOPED THIS YEAR ARE:

- To sand and finish a pair of wooden knitting needles
- To continue to develop knitting skills introduced in 1st grade
- To learn how to cast on and cast off their knitting
- To learn to purl
- To learn to crochet
- To learn to sew in ends in a knitting project
- To learn to sew on a button
- To learn to wet felt
- To learn to shape their knitting with "knit 2 together"
- To learn to sew up and stuff a project

TIME LINE OF PROJECTS: (Class is held 2 times a week for 50 minutes each)

August-December
- Sand and finish knitting needles with beeswax
- Flute case
- Folded paper star

January-June
- Gnome
- Sitting Kitty
- Bunny
- Rooster, Hen and Chick
- Squirrel
- Mouse
- Felted Egg

The second grade is full of joy. Rhythmic, repetitive activity with the hands strengthens the will and brings clearer thinking in adolescent years. Making things independently at a young age develops the powers of invention and creative thinking, which will, with continued use, increase with maturity.

¼" diameter hardwood dowels, cut to 9" lengths, 2/student
100-grit sandpaper
220-grit sandpaper
Beeswax
Rags for buffing
2 beads with 1/4" holes to fit the dowels
White glue
Sharpie marker

Write the student's name one inch from the end of each dowel. Sand the other end of each dowel into a tapered point with the 100-grit sandpaper. Support the dowel with your index finger while sanding. Make sure the point is long and gradually tapers to a gentle point, like a long tall gnome hat.

Sand the entire needle with the 220-sandpaper until it is as smooth as silk.

Coat the sanded needle all over with beeswax.

Use the rag to buff the needle until it is smooth.

Glue one bead onto the end of each dowel. Let dry before using.

Materials: Brown Sheep Lamb's Pride Worsted: 2 colors: 1 light and 1 dark
Knitting Needles size 8
Yarn Needle
Button
Thread
Sewing needle

With dark yarn: Cast on 20 stitches; knit 16 rows.

Stripes:
With light yarn: knit 1 row, purl 1 row (stockinette stitch.)
With dark yarn: knit 1 row, purl 1 row (stockinette stitch.)
Continue in stockinette stripes for a total of 8 stripes - 4 light, 4 dark – 16 rows.

With light yarn: knit 16 rows

Repeat stockinette stitch stripes reversing colors: start with dark color

With dark yarn: knit until the flute case measures 12". Bind off 10 stitches at the beginning of the next row. 10 stitches left.

Knit 4 rows plain.

Knit 2 together at the beginning of each row until 1 stitch remains.

With the remaining loop, finger knit 10 times. Break the yarn leaving a 6" tail.

Thread the yarn tail into yarn needle, and sew into the first finger knitting stitch, creating a loop. Sew in all yarn ends.

Fold the flute case in half, starting with the cast on edge and matching yarn, sew edges together with whipstitch. Try to match the stripes. Fasten off the yarn with 3 small stitches and sew in the yarn tail.

Fold the button flap over and figure out the button placement. Sew the button on with needle and thread.

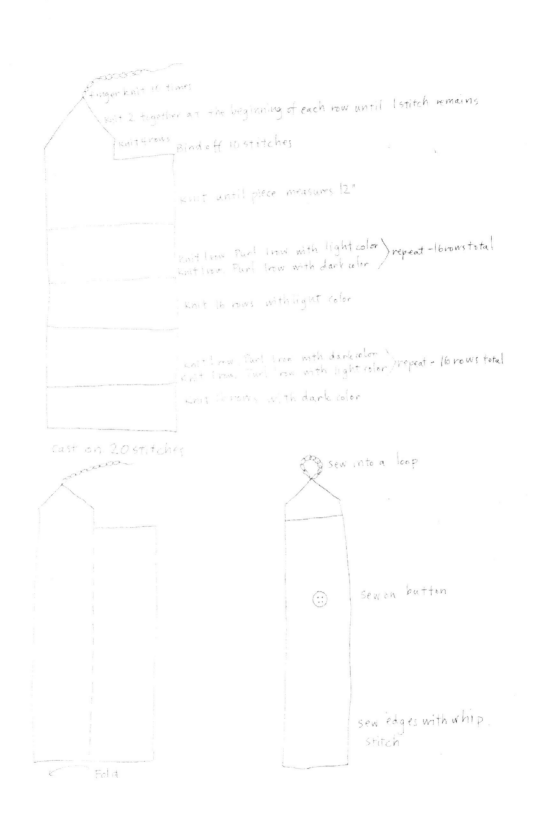

finger knit 6 times

knit 2 together at the beginning of each row until 1 stitch remains

knit 4 rows

Bind off 10 stitches

knit until piece measures 12"

knit 1 row, Purl 1 row with light color ⎫
knit 1 row, Purl 1 row with dark color ⎬ repeat - 16 rows total

knit 16 rows with light color

knit 1 row, Purl 1 row with dark color ⎫
knit 1 row, Purl 1 row with light color ⎬ repeat - 16 rows total

knit 16 rows with dark color

cast on 20 stitches

sew into a loop

Sew on button

sew edges with whip stitch

Fold

Knitting Worsted in Colors for: 1) Boots
                                     2) Pants
                                     3) Sweater
                                     4) Skin Tone-a natural skin tone
                                     5) Hat Color

Knitting Needles-Size 8
Crochet Hook-Size H
Yarn Needle
Wool Fleece for Stuffing

First Boot:
 With the boot color, cast on 12 stitches. Knit 10 rows. Break the yarn and join the pants color

Pants:
 Work in stockinette stitch-knit one row, purl one row for 6 rows. Break the yarn

Second Boot:
 With the boot color, cast on 12 stitches. Knit 10 rows. Break the yarn and join the pants color

Pants:
 Work in stockinette stitch-knit one row, purl one row for 6 rows. Arrange the two legs so they are both on one needle with the right sides facing you. Knit across both pants legs-24 stitches. Continue working across all stitches in stockinette stitch-knit one row, purl one row, beginning with a knit row, for 6 rows total. Break the yarn and join the sweater color

Sweater:
 Knit for 20 rows. Break the yarn and join the skin color.

Head:
With the skin color, work for 18 rows in stockinette stitch.
Head decrease: Row 1: *Knit 2 together, knit 3* repeat from* across row; knit to the end of the row.

Row 2 and all even numbered rows: Purl 1 row

Row 3: *Knit 2 together, knit 2* repeat from* across row; knit to the end of the row.

Row 5: *Knit 2 together, knit 1* repeat from* across row; knit to the end of the row.

Row 7: *Knit 2 together* repeat from* across row; knit to the end of the row.

Break the yarn 12" from the work and thread it onto a yarn needle. Pull the remaining stitches off the knitting needle and run the needle through the remaining loops beginning at the side away from the yarn end. Pull together tightly to gather. Fold the gnome in half and sew down the back of the head with a whipstitch. Stop at the sweater. Sew in all the yarn ends.

Sewing the pants:
Fold leg 1 in half and using the boot color yarn and a yarn needle, begin at the fold and sew up the boot. Change to pant color yarn and sew up the pants. Repeat sewing for leg 2. Sew the back of the pants together.

Stuff firmly with fleece. Make sure to get all the way into the toes. Sew up the sweater with sweater color yarn.

Neck:
With skin color yarn, thread a yarn needle with 12" of yarn. Begin at the back seam on the row above the sweater, sew a running stitch around the neck. Pull tightly and knot to the beginning of the yarn. Sew in all ends.

Arms:
With the sweater color yarn, cast on 12 stitches and knit 18 rows. Break the yarn and join the Skin color yarn.

Hands:
knit 1 row, purl 1 row
Hand decrease: Row 1: *Knit 2 together, knit 3* repeat from* across row; knit to the end of the row.

Row 2 and all even numbered rows: Purl 1 row
Row 3: *Knit 2 together, knit 2* repeat from* across row; knit to the end of the row.

Row 5: *Knit 2 together, knit 1* repeat from* across row; knit to the end of the row.

Row 7: *Knit 2 together* repeat from* across row; knit to the end of the row.

Break the yarn 12" from the work and thread onto a yarn needle. Pull the remaining stitches off the knitting needle and run the yarn needle through the remaining loops beginning at the side away from the yarn. Pull together tightly to gather.
Repeat for the second arm.

Sewing the arms:

Fold arm 1 in half and using skin color yarn and a yarn needle, begin at the fold and sew the hand. Change to the sweater color yarn and sew up the arms. Repeat for arm 2. Stuff the arms with fleece.

Position the arms at the sides of the body, right below the neck yarn, and sew onto the body.

Hat:

With the crochet hook and the hat color yarn, pull up a loop of yarn at the head seam at the back of the head and join with a slipstitch. Go under a knit stitch, pull up a loop, and make a single crochet. Continue around the head, going higher in the front of the head and lower to meet the first stitch at the back. On the second and following rows, work into the previous row. Continue working in rounds into each single crochet around and around the head. As the hat reaches above the head begin to decrease by skipping every 6th single crochet. Work until there are only a few single crochets in each round. Break the yarn and pull the yarn through the loop. Sew in all ends.

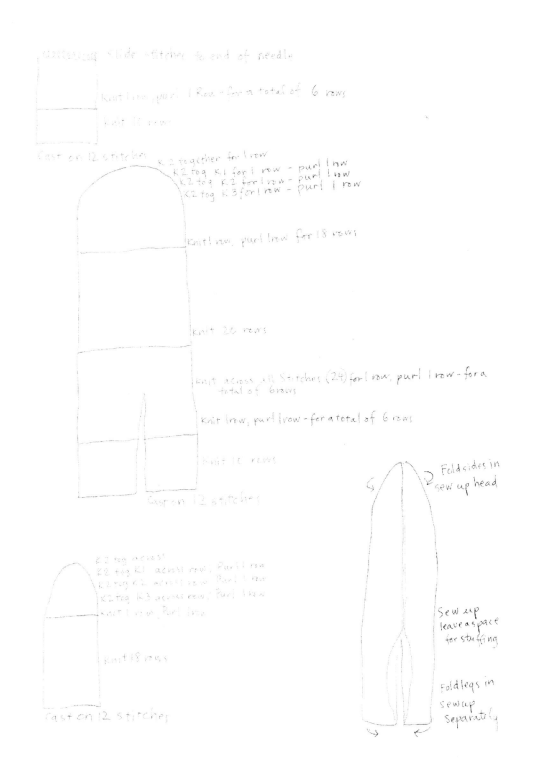

Decreasing - slide stitches to end of needle

Knit 1 row, purl 1 Row - for a total of 6 rows

knit 10 rows

Cast on 12 stitches

K 2 together for 1 row
K2 tog K1 for 1 row - purl 1 row
K2 tog K2 for 1 row - purl 1 row
K2 tog K3 for 1 row - purl 1 row

knit 1 row, purl 1 row for 18 rows

knit 26 rows

knit across all stitches (24) for 1 row, purl 1 row - for a total of 6 rows

knit 1 row, purl 1 row - for a total of 6 rows

knit 10 rows

Cast on 12 stitches

K2 tog across
K2 tog K1 across row, Purl 1 row
K2 tog K2 across row, Purl 1 row
K2 tog K3 across row, Purl 1 row
Knit 1 row, Purl 1 row

knit 18 rows

Cast on 12 stitches

Fold sides in
sew up head

Sew up
leave a space
for stuffing

Fold legs in
sew up
separately

Knitting Worsted Yarn, Brown Sheep, Lamb's pride-grey
Knitting Needles-Size 8
Yarn Needle
Wool Fleece for Stuffing

Body:
Cast on 20 stitches
Knit 10 rows –Garter Stitch- 5 ridges on a side
Change to Stockinette Stitch- Knit 1 row, Purl 1 row for 20 rows.
Bind off leaving an 18" tail for sewing up

Fold the body in half and using the tail left from casting on, sew up the long edge and across the top. Knot the yarn but leave the yarn tail.
Stuff firmly with fleece.

To define the neck, attach a piece of yarn at the seam about halfway through the stockinette section. Sew a running stitch under one stitch, over one stitch around to form the neck. Pull tightly and knot to the yarn tail.

Using the yarn tail left from sewing up the sides, take a large stitch in the center of the head to form the ears.
Sew in yarn tails.

Tail:
Cast on 20 stitches. Knit in stockinette stitch-knit 1 row, purl 1 row, for 6 rows. Bind off.
Sew cast on and bind off edges together.
Sew onto the garter stitch section at the back of the cat.

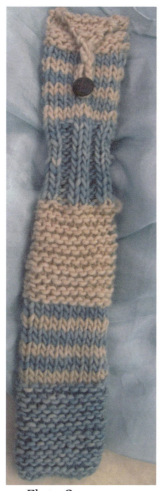

Flute Case

Gnome

Sitting-up Kitty

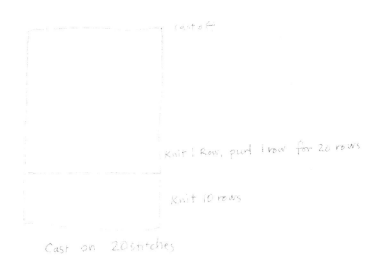

cast off

Knit 1 Row, purl 1 row for 20 rows

Knit 10 rows

Cast on 20 stitches

Fold in half
Sew up side and top

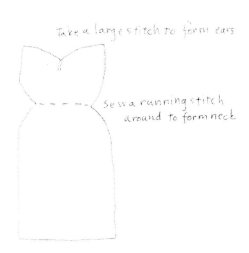

Take a large stitch to form ears

Sew a running stitch
around to form neck

Knitting Worsted Yarn, Brown Sheep, Lamb's Pride-white, grey or fawn
Knitting Needles-Size 8
Yarn Needle
Wool Fleece for Stuffing and tail
Needle
Thread

Body:
Cast on 20 Stitches.
Knit in stockinette stitch, (knit one row, purl one row) until you have a square, about 40 rows. End with a purl row.
Bind off

Sewing up:
Head:
With the yarn needle and an 18" piece of yarn, sew a circle on one side, centered and reaching about ½ way across the square, with running stitch. Pull the ends together and stuff to form the head. Knot firmly.

Legs:
Fold one corner near the head on the diagonal and sew from the corner about ½ way up one side. Sew the other front leg.
Sew back legs in a similar fashion leaving the tummy partially open to stuff. Stuff with fleece and sew up.
Fold the back legs forward and tack to the sides of the body.

Ears:
Cast on 3 stitches. Knit 10 rows.
Knit 2 together, knit 1.
Next row, knit 2 together. Cut the yarn
Make two.

Sew ears to the top of head.

Tail:
Roll a small ball from the wool fleece
Take several stitches through the ball of fleece and sew in the appropriate place.

Bunny

Cast off

Knit until a square

Cast on 20 stitches

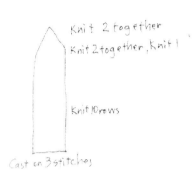

Knit 2 together

Knit 2 together, Knit 1

Knit 10 rows

Cast on 3 stitches

Sewing up:

Head:

Running Stitch

Legs: Point 1 - Fold A to B - sew edge
Point 2 - Fold A to C - sew edge
Point 3 - Fold D to E - sew edge
Point 4 - Fold D to F - sew edge

Knitting Worsted Yarn, Brown Sheep, Lamb's Pride-white, buff, brown or rust
Small amount of red for the comb, yellow for the beak and different colors for the
rooster's tail
Knitting Needles-Size 8
Yarn Needle
Wool Fleece for Stuffing
Crochet Hook size H
Wooden beads for hanging

Rooster, (Hen, Chick) Body:
Cast on 25 (20, 15) stitches.
Knit in stockinette stitch, (knit one row, purl one row) until you have a square. End
with a purl row.
Bind off

Sewing up:
Fold along the diagonal to form a triangle. Sew up along one side; stuff; sew up the
second side.

Wings:
Cast on 6 stitches, knit 10 rows
Row 1: Knit 2 Together, knit to the end of the row
Row 2: Knit
Repeat rows 1 & 2 until 1 stitch is left. Pull yarn through the final loop.
Make 2.
Determine the front of the chicken; sew the wings onto the sides of the chicken.

Beak:
With the yellow yarn and the crochet hook, attach the yarn where the beak should
be; Chain 4, (3,3) stitches; turn work a single crochet into the second chain from the
hook. Work one single crochet into each chain. Cut the yarn and pull through the
loop. Sew in ends.

Comb:
 With the red yarn, pull up a loop with the crochet hook along the hen's or rooster's
head; work 3-4 single crochets along the top of the head; chain 1, turn work. Work
one single crochet into each single crochet. Cut the yarn, pull through the loop and
sew in the ends.

To string the chickens:
Attach a 36"piece of yarn to the chick's back; knot firmly, sew in end. String a few
beads onto the yarn to space the chickens. With a yarn needle threaded onto the
yarn, run the yarn up through the lower point of the chicken coming out between
the wings, knot the yarn. String a few beads onto the yarn to space the chickens.

Repeat for the rooster. Tie a loop onto the top of the yarn to hang.

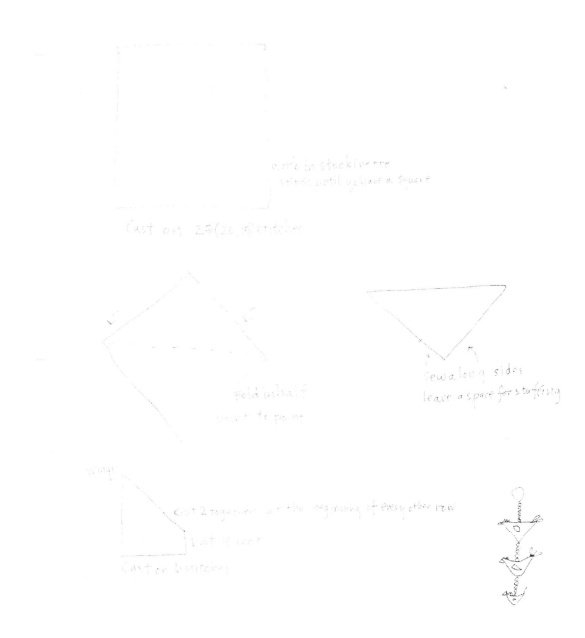

work in stockinette
stitch until you have a square

Cast on 28(20, 16) stitches

Fold in half
point to point

Sew along sides
leave a space for stuffing

wing

Knit 2 together at the beginning of every other row

Cast 6 over

Cast on 14 stitches

Knitting, Brown Sheep Lamb's pride Worsted Weight Yarn -grey or reddish brown
Knitting Needles-Size 8
Yarn Needle
Wool Fleece for Stuffing
2"x 3" Piece of Cardboard

Body:
Cast on 25 Stitches.
Work in stockinette stitch, (knit one row, purl one row) for 42 rows or until you have a square. End with a purl row.

Head:
Row 1: cast off 6 stitches, knit to the end of the row.
Row 2: cast off 6 stitches, purl to the end of the row.
Continuing in stockinette stitch, work until the head is a square, about 16 rows. Bind off.

Sewing up:
Head:
With the yarn needle and an 18" piece of yarn, fold the head in half and sew the top of the head together. Sew a running stitch around the front of the head. Pull the ends together and stuff to form the head.

Legs:
Fold one corner near the head on the diagonal and sew from the corner about ½ way up one side. Sew the other front leg.
Sew the back legs in a similar fashion leaving the tummy partially open to stuff. Stuff with fleece and sew up.

Ears:
Cast on 3 stitches. Knit 2 rows.
Knit 2 together, knit 1.
Next row knit 2 stitches together. End yarn
Make two.

Sew the ears to the top of the head.

Tail:
Using the 2" by 4" piece of cardboard, wrap the yarn around the 2" width until the card is covered. The thicker the yarn, the thicker the tail will be. With the yarn needle threaded with yarn, sew a backstitch up the center of the card, making sure to catch all the yarns in at least one stitch. Sew along both sides of the card. Slide the yarn off the card. Match up the backstitch seams and sew the two sides together

along the backstitch seam. Clip loops 1" away from the center seam on either side of the tail. Sew onto the Squirrel in the appropriate place.

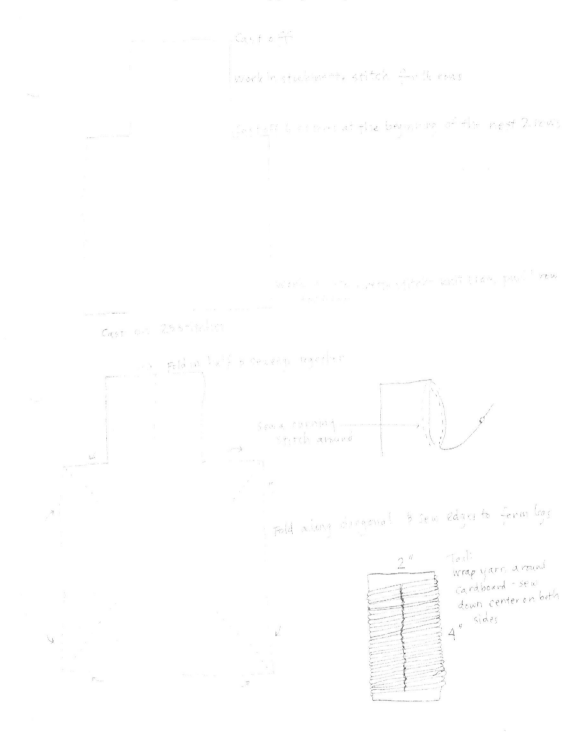

Brown Sheep Lamb's pride Worsted Weight Yarn, -grey or white for the mouse
body; dark brown yarn for the eyes and nose
Knitting Needles-Size 8
Yarn Needle
Wool Fleece for Stuffing
Dark brown Embroidery thread
Embroidery Needle

Body:
Cast on 20 Stitches.
Work in stockinette stitch, (knit one row, purl one row) for 6 rows. End with a purl
row.
Row 1: Knit 2 together, knit to the last two stitches, Knit 2 together.
Row 2: Purl
Repeat Rows 1 and 2 until 2 stitches are left
Next row: knit 2 together, cut yarn and pull the yarn through the loop.

Sewing up:
With the yarn needle and an 18" piece of yarn, fold the body in half lengthwise and
sew the sides together; leave the cast on edge open.
Stuff with fleece and sew a running stitch around the cast on edge.
Pull the ends together, tie and sew in.

Ears:
Finger knit about an inch
Make two.

Sew the ears to top of the head: Attach one end of the finger knitting to the head.
Attach the other end of the finger knitting about ½" away. Knot firmly.

Tail:
Finger knit for 3". Sew onto the mouse in the appropriate place.

Eyes:
With the dark yarn, come from the back of the head about an inch away from where
the eyes belong. Pull the yarn until the end pops inside the mouse; sew a stitch of
yarn. Bring the needle to the location of the second eye. Sew a stitch of yarn and
take the yarn out the back of the head.

Nose:
With the dark yarn, take 3 stitches at the pointed tip of the mouse.

Whiskers:

With embroidery thread, take a stitch next to the nose; hold your finger so the yarn wraps around it as the thread is pulled, leaving a loop. Make a small stitch at the base of the loop. Repeat looping stitch on the same side, move to the other side and make two looping stitches. Knot the yarn. Cut the loops.

knit 2 together at the beginning of each knit row

work 6 rows in Stockinette stitch (knit/row purl row)

sew up

fold →

Bunny

Mouse

Squirrel

Opening:
From as far as the stars
To here where I stand
I've come to use my right and left hands;
To card, to spin,
To crochet and to stitch.
For such fine work,
My hands are fit.

Crochet:
Under the bridge of two,
Catch a fish and pull it through,
Now you have two.
Catch it again
And pull it in.

Closing:
My work for now is over,
My hands for now must rest.
I thank you hands,
Both right and left,
For helping me to do my best.

Lesson Plan for Handwork

Grade three:
THE GOALS FOR THIS YEAR ARE:
- To form good habits in taking care of work and materials
- To foster an appreciation for natural materials
- To begin to develop a sense of color
- To learn to be self-sufficient and feel that "I can do"
- To become aware of the quality of their work
- To foster an appreciation of where fiber comes from
- To introduce the process of processing wool- from animal to finished object
- To introduce natural dyeing

THE MAIN SKILLS TO BE INTRODUCED AND FURTHER DEVELOPED THIS YEAR ARE:
- To wet felt a ball
- To introduce embroidery
- To introduce the use of the thimble
- To continue to develop crocheting
- To experience unwashed wool from a sheep
- To learn to wash, card, dye and spin wool
- To make a wooden spindle
- To learn to weave on a frame loom
- To learn double crochet

TIME LINE OF PROJECTS: (Class is held 2 times a week for 50 minutes each)
August-October
- River ball- wet felting and embroidery
November-January
- Crocheted animal hand puppet-snake, horse etc...
February
- Crocheted hat
March-April
- Introduction to Wool
- Wash Wool
- Card Wool
- Make drop spindles
- Spin Wool
- Weave Pencil Case on the frame loom
May-June
- Recorder Case
- Water bottle carrier
- Washcloth
- Hot pad
- Woggily Book Mark
- Double Crochet Hot Pat
- Granny Square Bag

Generally, children in the third grade experience the nine-year change. Children realize that they are separate beings. They begin to see both subjective and objective viewpoints. The nine-year change can be a painful separation, marked by moodiness and challenging behavior. Fairness becomes very important. They leave behind the feelings of magic and glow. The curtain has parted. They leave paradise and come onto the Earth. Life becomes ordinary.

To address these events, they study farming, shelter and clothing. They become aware of laws versus mistakes and develop reverence for and confidence in the real world. Within the farming and shelter blocks, they study fibers, weaving, spinning and measurement. They look into responsibility and service. They are ready for more problem solving. The third grade curriculum is grounding and gives them the basis for the nine-year change. The 3rd grade curriculum prepares the students for the 10th grade weaving curriculum. The two units are seven years apart. Third graders are at the same relative stage in the second seven-year cycle as they will be in the third seven-year cycle in 10th grade.

Often the class teacher will ask if the handwork teacher can help the students with a weaving project. Weaving round and round on a card loom can create a small bag that can be closed with a button. Alternatively, weaving on a simple peg loom, students can make a hot pad or mat for home use. They card, spin, wash and dye wool and include the yarn in the weaving project. As the yarn is spun and prepared for dyeing students learn to make a skein and to tie overhand and figure 8 knots. The words warp and weft are introduced. Students may use either their fingers or a yarn needle to weave. The students pack the yarn with their fingers. The process of spinning yarn and weaving a project introduces the student to the complete process from fiber, hopefully with the shearing of the fleece, processing, carding, spinning the wool into yarn, weaving the yarn into a textile and finally, finishing the project. Seeing the complete process meets the needs of the third grader experiencing the 9-year change as they fall out of heaven. The third grade student is now ready to understand the mechanism and technology of the world.

Carded Wool Fleece (make sure it felts by first felting a tiny piece into a little ball)
Dish tub
Warm water
Dish soap
Perle Cotton size 5 or 8 in Blue, Green, Yellow, Orange, Red and Purple
Embroidery or chenille Needle
Thimble

Ball:

Start with a strip of fleece, 3" wide by 18" long. Roll the fleece into a ball that fits into your hand; add more fleece if necessary. The larger the ball the longer it will take to felt. Fill the tub with warm water and a squirt of dish soap. Add enough soap until the water feels slippery. Hold the fleece ball in your hand and slowly lower it into the water, keeping your hand under the ball. Lift the ball out and let the water drip back into the tub. Pass the fleece ball back and forth from hand to hand until the ball begins to feel slightly firmer. Begin to roll the ball between your palms, not pressing at all, just gently rolling the ball. As the ball becomes firmer, additional pressure can be used. If the ball deforms in shape, use gentler pressure. Eventually, great pressure can be exerted on the ball. When it no longer compresses and it feels very firm, rinse it under clear water and squeeze it until no more soap runs out. Roll the ball between your palms to reshape it into a sphere. Set on a screen to dry.

Embroidery:

Once the ball is dry, it can be embroidered. Begin with the Blue perle cotton. Thread the needle and take a stitch about 1" long into the ball. Pull the thread until it just pops into the fleece. Sew a winding river around the ball using outline stitch. Use the thimble to push the needle through the fleece. End the blue "river" where it started. Sew around the ball once more with blue, stitching right next to the first row of stitching. End the thread by sewing a long stitch, about 1", going in a different direction than previous stitching. Cut the thread close to where it exits the ball. You have sewn the river. Next sew the riverbanks with green. Then add the flowers, Yellow, orange, red and purple. Continue stitching right up against the last round until the entire ball is covered with stitching. A length of thread can be added to hang the ball.

Materials: Brown Sheep Lamb's Pride Worsted Weight Yarn in Red, Dark Brown, and light Yellow, a small bit of white
Stitch Marker
Crochet Hook size H
Yarn Darning Needle

With the Red Yarn, crochet a chain long enough to go around your hand, about 38 stitches. Join to the first chain. Place marker.

Single crochet in each chain around continuing to move the marker each round for 5 rounds.

Change to dark brown yarn and continue to work around in single crochet for 4 rounds

Change to yellow yarn and continue to work around in single crochet for 4 rounds

Change to dark brown yarn and continue to work around in single crochet for 3 rounds

Change to red yarn and continue to work around in single crochet for 4 rounds

On the next round chain 14 stitches, single crochet into the 15th single crochet from the beginning of the chain-the space for the lower jaw created. Continue to single crochet around until you reach the chain. Make 1 single crochet in each chain stitch. Continue around in single crochet for 2 more rounds.

Begin Decreasing:
 At the beginning of the next round, Single crochet 6, skip 1 single crochet in the previous round (decrease made); Continue Single crochet 6, skip 1 around. The snake snout should begin to gradually taper to a point. When there are only 6 single crochets left in a round, pull up a loop in each stitch and keep them on the hook, break the yarn 6 inches from the last single crochet and thread it onto a yarn needle. Run the needle through the loops and pull tightly. Pull the yarn to the inside of the work and sew under.

Lower jaw:
 Join the red yarn at the corner of the space created by the 14 chains. Make one single crochet into each chain and each skipped single crochet: 28 single crochets. Continue to single crochet around decreasing every 7th stitch as for the snout. Fasten off as above when 6 single crochets remain.

Tongue:

Pick up 5 single crochets inside the mouth for the tongue. Chain 2, turn work. Continue single crochet and turning for a total of 8 rows. Crochet 2, turn, for 3 rows, crochet 2 together, and fasten yarn off. Repeat for the other side of the tongue.

Eyes:
Chain 6 with the dark brown yarn; join into a ring by slip stitching to the first chain. Make 6 single crochets into the center of the ring. Cut the yarn. Join the white yarn, work 2 single crochets in each single crochet around-12 single crochets. Fasten off. Repeat for the other eye. Sew the eyes into place. Sew in all yarn ends.

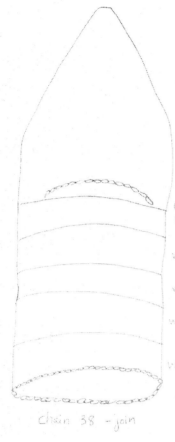

Begin decreasing - work 6 SC - skip 1 - repeat around

work 2 rounds

Work 1 round including chain stitches

chain 14 join and continue single crochet in 15th sc from hook

Work 4 rounds Red

work 4 rounds Dk Brown

work 4 rounds Yellow

work 4 rounds Dk Brown

work 5 rounds red

chain 38 - join

- Eyes - chain 6; join
  6 single crochets into
  the center
  2 single crochets in
  each single crochet
  around

River Ball   River Ball

Snake Puppet

-Knitting Worsted in a horse color, a nose color and dark brown or black for the eyes
-Stitch Markers
-Crochet hook-size H
-2 Sewing Pins
-Yarn needle

Chain 36
Join into a ring by slip stitching into the first chain, place marker
Work single crochet for 18 rounds.
Next round make the mouth opening: Chain 18; skip 18 single crochets; single crochet in the next single crochet; single crochet to the end of the round.
Continue working in the round for 14 rounds
Nose round 1: *Single crochet in each of the next 5 single crochets, skip the next single crochet*, Repeat between *'s around
Nose round 2: *Single crochet in each of the next 4 single crochets, skip the next single crochet*, Repeat between *'s around
Nose round 3: *Single crochet in each of the next 3 single crochets, skip the next single crochet*, Repeat between *'s around
Nose round 4: *Single crochet in each of the next 2 single crochets, skip the next single crochet*, Repeat between *'s around
Nose round 5: *Work one single crochet, skip the next single crochet*, Repeat between *'s around
Break yarn leaving a 12" tail
With the yarn needle, sew through 6 single crochets around; pull the yarn tightly to gather. Pull the yarn through to the inside and knot. Sew in all ends.

Lower Jaw:
Round 1: Single crochet 36 single crochets around the mouth opening
Round 2: Skip 1 single crochet; single crochet 17, place marker; skip 1 single crochet; single crochet 17, place marker.
Round 3-10: Skip 1 single crochet; single crochet to the marker; skip 1 single crochet; single crochet to the marker.
Break the yarn leaving a 12" tail
With the yarn needle, sew through 6 single crochets around; pull the yarn tightly to gather. Pull the yarn through to the inside and knot. Sew all ends in.

Ears, make 2:
Chain 4; Turn; * skip the first chain, work 3 single crochets, chain 1, turn work.
Rows 2-4 *Work 3 single crochets, chain 1, turn work.
Row 5: single crochet 1, skip the next single crochet, single crochet 1, chain 1, turn work
Row 6: Pull up a loop in the first single crochet, Pull up a loop in the second single crochet, Pull the yarn through both loops. Sew in all yarn ends. Sew the ears in place on the head.

Mane:

Cut yarn into 3"-5" lengths. Put the crochet hook under two loops on the top of the head slightly in front of the ears, fold a length of yarn in half, pull a loop of yarn through, pull the ends of the yarn through the loop. Repeat down the horse's neck to create the mane.

Nose:

Using the pinkish nose yarn, stitch several long stitches to create the nose.

Eyes:

Mark the eye location on either side of the head with sewing pins. With dark brown yarn, make several long stitches at the sewing pins for the eyes.

Brown Sheep Lamb's Pride Knitting Worsted: Purple and other colors
Crochet Hook size H
Yarn Needle
Split ring marker

With the purple yarn, chain 6. Make a ring by slip stitching through the first chain and the loop on the hook.

Round 1: Make 6 single crochets into the middle of the ring; place a marker in the last single crochet

Round 2: Make 2 single crochets into each single crochet around: 12 single crochets; move marker to the last single crochet

Round 3: *Make 1 single crochet in the first single crochet; make 2 single crochets into the next single crochet * repeat around: 18 single crochets; move marker to the last single crochet

Round 4: *Make 1 single crochet in each of the next two single crochets; make 2 single crochets into the next single crochet (increase)* repeat around: 24 single crochets; move marker to the last single crochet

Rounds 5 and on: Continue to increase 6 single crochets each round by increasing the single crochets between the increases. Work until the disc covers the top of the head, about 5"-6" in diameter.

If the hat grows too fast and begins to ruffle, skip a single crochet every 10 single crochets for a round or two.

If the hat is not growing fast enough, increase more often.
Once the crown is the right size work the next round and all future rounds to the end as follows: work 1 single crochet in each single crochet around. Change colors as desired, hide the ends inside of the crochet as you work by holding the ends on top of the work and crocheting around them.

Try the hat on frequently to see if it fits. When it comes halfway down your ears, you can slip stitch into the final stitch. Sew in all yarn ends.

Enjoy your hat!

Cotton worsted weight yarn
Crochet Hook size H
Yarn Needle
Split Ring Marker
Water Bottle

With the yarn, chain 6. Make a ring by pulling a loop through the first chain and the loop on the hook.

Round 1: Make 6 single crochets into the middle of the ring; place the marker in the last single crochet

Round 2: Make 2 single crochets into each single crochet around: 12 single crochets; move the marker to the last single crochet

Round 3: *Make 1 single crochet in the first single crochet; make 2 single crochets into the next single crochet * repeat from* around: 18 single crochets; move the marker to the last single crochet

Round 4: *Make 1 single crochet in each of the next two single crochets; make 2 single crochets into the next single crochet (increase)* repeat from* around: 24 single crochets; move the marker to the last single crochet

Rounds 5 and on: Continue to increase 6 single crochets each round by increasing the number of single crochets between the increases.

Work until the disc is the size of the base of the water bottle.

Work one single crochet into each single crochet around without increasing until the work measures 1" above the base.

Next round: *Chain 4, skip 4 single crochets, single crochet in the next single crochet* repeat from * around to the first chain.

Next round and on: *Chain 4, single crochet into the next chain 4 loop from the row below* repeat from*. Continue chaining and single crocheting into loops until the piece reaches the top of the water bottle. Slip stitch into the next chain. Sew in yarn ends.

Make a chain 18" long. Thread it through the loops in the second row from the top of the bag. Tie the ends together.
Insert the water bottle.

See rubber bottle or dish if it is big enough

crochet without increasing parts

chain 4 single crochet in 5th single crochet

chain 4 single crochet in 4 chain loop

Brown Sheep Lamb's Pride Worsted Weight yarn in several colors
Crochet Hook size H
Yarn Needle
Split ring marker

With the yarn, chain 6. Make a ring by pulling a loop through the first chain and the loop on the hook.

Round 1: Make 6 single crochets into the middle of the ring; place the marker in the last single crochet

Round 2: Make 2 single crochets into each single crochet around: 12 single crochets; move the marker to the last single crochet

Round 3: *Make 1 single crochet in the first single crochet; make 2 single crochets into the next single crochet * repeat around: 18 single crochets.

Round 4: Make 1 single crochet into each single crochet in the round before. Continue around until piece measures 12". Place marker.

Round A: *work 2 single crochets into each single crochet in the row before* repeat around to marker.

Repeat Round A for 2 more rounds.

Slip stitch into the next single crochet. Sew in all yarn ends.

Make a chain 18" long. With the yarn needle thread the chain through the space between every 2 single crochets in the last row before Round A. Tie ends together.

Cotton knitting worsted in off white and blue
Crochet Hook size H
Yarn Needle

Washcloth: Chain 32.

Row 1: Make 1 single crochet in the 3rd chain from the hook. Single crochet in each chain; 30 single crochets. Chain 2(turning chain); turn work.

Row 2: skip chain 2 turning chain and make 1 single crochet in each single crochet; chain 2. Turn work.

Repeat Row 2 until the work is a square. To determine a square, lay the work flat and without stretching, fold the lower right corner diagonally across the work. When it reaches up to the upper left corner, it is a square.

End the final row without making a turning chain. Cut the yarn and pull through the loop.

Edging:
With the blue yarn, pull a loop up along the edge of the square; chain 1. Work single crochets around the edges of the square, 1 single crochet in each single crochet or row. When a corner is reached, work 3 single crochets in the corner stitch. To make a loop in one corner: work first corner stitch, chain 10, work last corner stitch. Continue around washcloth until the first chain is reached. Slip stitch into the first chain. Cut the yarn and pull through the loop.

Sew in all yarn ends.

Repeat Row 2 until work is a square

Row 2 - skip chain 2 - single crochet
across

chain 32 - turn - single crochet in 3rd chain from hook
single crochet across - 30 single crochets

work 3 chains in each corner

Cotton worsted weight yarn in 2 colors
Crochet Hook size H
Yarn Needle

Sides, make 2: Chain 32.

Row 1: Make 1 single crochet in the 3rd chain from the hook. Single crochet in each chain across; 30 single crochets. Chain 2(turning chain); turn work.

Row 2: skip chain 2 turning chain and make 1 single crochet in each single crochet; chain 2. Turn work.

Repeat Row 2 until the work is a square. To determine a square, lay the work flat and without stretching, fold the lower right corner diagonally across the work. When it reaches up to the upper left corner, it is a square.

End the final row without making a turning chain. Cut the yarn and pull through the loop.

Edging:
Lay one square on top of the other. With contrasting yarn, pull a loop up through the edges of both squares; chain 1. Work single crochets around the edge, 1 single crochet in each single crochet or row going through both squares. When a corner is reached, work 3 single crochets in the corner stitches. To make a loop in one corner: work first corner stitch, chain 10, work last corner stitch. Continue around the hot pad until the first chain is reached. Slip stitch into the first chain. Cut the yarn and pull through the loop.

Sew in all yarn ends.

Knitting worsted including novelty yarns, good way to use up scraps
Crochet Hook size H
Yarn Needle

Chain 9.

Row 1: skip first 2 chains, double crochet into the 3rd chain from the hook. Double crochet into each chain across, 7 double crochets. Chain 2; turn work.

Row 2: skip first 2 chains. Double crochet into each double crochet across, 7 double crochets. Chain 2; turn work.

Repeat row 2 until work measures 4"

Ruffle:
Row 1: Work 2 double crochets into each double crochet across, 14 double crochets. Chain 2; turn work.

Row 2: Work 2 double crochets into each double crochet across, 28 double crochets. Cut the yarn and pull through the loop.

Sew in ends.
Novelty yarns work well for the ruffle.

Cotton knitting worsted in yellow, orange & red
Crochet Hook size H
Yarn Needle

To make ring: With yellow yarn, Chain 6. Join to first chain.

Round 1: Chain 2 (counts as first double crochet); Work 11 Double Crochets into the ring. Slip stitch to the original chain. Chain 2.

Round 2: Chain 2 (counts as first double crochet); Work 1 double crochet into the original chain in round one. Work 2 double crochets into each double crochet around-24 double crochets. Change to orange yarn.

Round 3: Chain 2 (counts as first double crochet); *Work 2 double crochets into the first double crochet, work 1 double crochet into the next double crochet* Repeat around between *'s. 36 double crochets.

Round 4: Chain 2 (counts as first double crochet); *Work 2 double crochets into the first double crochet, Work 1 double crochet into each of the next 2 double crochets* Repeat between *'s around. 48 double crochets.

Round 5: Chain 2 (counts as first double crochet); *Work 2 double crochets into the first double crochet, Work 1 double crochet into each of the next 3 double crochets* Repeat between *'s around. 60 double crochets. Change to red yarn.

Round 6: Chain 2 (counts as first double crochet); *Work 2 double crochets into the first double crochet, Work 1 double crochet into each of the next 4 double crochets* Repeat between *'s around. 72 double crochets. Fold work in half.

Round 7: chain 2, Working through both layers, *Work 2 double crochets into the first double crochets, Work 1 double crochet into the next 5 double crochets* Repeat between *'s around. 42 double crochets. Chain 10; slip stitch to the same double crochet. Cut the yarn and pull through the loop.
Sew in all ends.

Knitting worsted yarn - small amounts of many colors
Crochet Hook size H
Yarn Needle
Button

Square, make 10:
Chain 6, slip stitch into the first chain to make a ring.

Round 1: Chain 3; make 2 double crochets into the ring; *chain 2; make 3 double crochets into the ring*Repeat between *'s 2 more times; chain 2; slip stitch to the first chain. Slip stitch to the next chain space or cut the yarn and pull through the loop if you want to change the yarn color.

*Round 2:*if using a new color join the yarn in a chain 2 space; for new color or old color: chain 3 (counts as 1 double crochet). In the same chain 2 space, work 1 double crochet; chain 2; still in the same chain 2 space work 2 double crochets. In the next chain 2 space work *2 double crochets, chain 2; 2 double crochets (corner made.)*Repeat between *'s 2 more times, slip stitch to the first chain. Slip stitch to the next chain 2 space or cut the yarn and pull through the loop if you want to change the yarn color.

Round 3: If using a new color join the yarn in a corner chain 2 space; for new color or old color: Chain 3 (counts as a 1 double crochet). In the same chain 2 space, work 1 double crochet; chain 2; still in the same chain 2 space work 2 double crochets. *Skip 2 double crochets, make 2 double crochets into the space after the 2nd double crochet. In the next chain 2 space work 2 double crochets, chain 2, 2 double crochets (corner made)*Repeat between *'s 2 more times; end: Skip 2 double crochets, make 2 double crochets into the space after the 2nd double crochet; slip stitch to the first chain. Slip stitch to the next chain 2 space or cut the yarn and pull through the loop if you want to change yarn color.

Round 4: If using a new color join yarn in a corner chain 2 space; for new color or old color: Chain 3 (counts as 1 double crochet). In the same chain 2 space, work 1 double crochet; chain 2; still in the same chain 2 space work 2 double crochets. Next: (* Skip 2 double crochets, make 2 double crochets into the space after the 2nd double crochet*repeat from* to *; in the next chain 2 space work 2 double crochets, chain 2; make 2 double crochets, corner made), repeat between ()'s 2 more times. End: *Skip 2 double crochets, make 2 double crochets into the space after the 2nd double crochet*repeat from*, slip stitch to the first chain. Cut the yarn and pull the yarn through the loop.

Sewing up:
Sew the granny squares into 2 larger squares of 4 squares each. Sew the larger squares together on 3 sides.

Washcloth

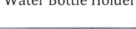
Water Bottle Holder

Recorder Case

Granny Square Bag

To make the flap, sew the remaining 2 squares together and sew to the open end of one large square. Sew the button onto the square below the flap. Make a chained loop on the flap to catch the button.

Strap:
Beginning 2 double crochets to the right of the side seam, work 4 double crochets into the edge of the bag; Chain 2; turn work.

Row 1: Work 1 double crochet in each double crochet; Chain 2; turn work.

Repeat row 1 until the strap goes over your shoulder, about 36".

Final row: To join the strap to the other side of the bag: holding the strap next to the bag, work 1 double crochet through a double crochet on the strap and a double crochet on the bag; repeat across the row. Cut the yarn and pull the yarn through the loop. Sew in all yarn ends.

Unwashed fleece from a sheep
Dish detergent
Large Tubs, at least 2
Drying racks, such as gardening flats

Sort through the fleece and remove any large pieces of vegetable matter. Pull off any tags (dung) from the edges of the fleece.

Look at the locks. Observe the crimp and waviness of the locks. Observe the changes in the color of the fleece from the cut end to the tip. Has the sun bleached the tips? Was it a white sheep or a multi-colored sheep? Is each fiber very tiny or thicker and more hair like?

Fill the tubs with water as hot as the students' hands can handle. The hotter the water is now, the cleaner the fleece will be later. Add enough dish detergent to one tub to make the water feel slippery. Suds don't matter. They will form as the fleece is washed. Pull off a handful of fleece, hold it by the cut end and swish the tips into the soapy water a few times. Change to hold the tips and swish the fleece in the soapy water again. Squeeze the soapy water back into the tub. Note if it has changed color. Now, swish the fleece into the clear water. Swish it vigorously. Hold the fleece by the other end and swish again. Squeeze the water into another tub or onto the garden. Not back into the rinse water! Spread the locks onto the drying racks or towels and let them dry. It may take several days to dry depending on the temperature and the weather. Wool can hold up to 30% of its weight in water!

Spindle

3" x 3" x 1/4" piece of Birch or Mahogany, either solid or ply- wood
Hand Drill with ¼" bit
9" length of ¼" Hardwood dowel
White or Wood Glue
220-grit sandpaper
Beeswax
Rag
1/8" screw-in hook

Whorl:
Drill a ¼" hole in the center of the 3"x3" wood. Sand the edges of the wood with the 220 sandpaper until smooth. Pay special attention to the edges and corners. When smooth, rub the beeswax onto the wood. Buff the wood with the rag until smooth.

Spindle:
Sand, wax and buff the dowel. Glue the whorl onto the dowel about 2" from one end of the dowel. Let dry.

Screw the hook into the short end of the dowel. It might work better if the hole is predrilled.

Carding Fleece

Dry Washed wool fleece
A pair of Hand Cards

Pull out a lock from the fleece. Spread out the fibers. Open up the tips. Note the cut end of the lock.
Hold one of the hand cards with the left palm facing you grasping the handle with the carding cloth below the handle. Pull the opened lock across the carding teeth and let it catch in the cloth. Repeat with more locks until the hand card has a thin layer of fleece over it.
Grasp the second Hand card with the right hand, teeth pointing down. Make a combing motion across the hand card in your left hand. Repeat until most of the fleece has transferred from the left hand card to the right hand card. Notice the straightness of the fibers.
Set the hand card down with the handle away from you. Roll the fleece out of the teeth of the carder into a tube or rolag.

The rolag is now ready for spinning.

Spinning

Spindle
Carded Rolags or roving

Practice motion: Sit in a chair, place the spindle on the thigh and push it along the leg.
Hook a bit of fleece from the rolag or roving on the hook. Holding the fleece at the hook, roll the spindle down the thigh. Let it spin off the knee. As it begins to slow down catch it between the knees or let it lay on the ground. Pull the fleece out with the right hand until just a few fibers are between the hands. Open the fingers holding the fiber at the hook. Watch the twist travel up into the fleece.
 Repeat rolling the spindle along the leg, pinching the yarn at the top of the twist, pulling the fleece out, (drafting) and pinching at the top of the new section. Let the twist wind up the fleece.
When the yarn becomes too long to work with comfortably, wind it onto the spindle by: first, unhooking the yarn from the hook and tying it around the spindle under the whorl. Second, wind the yarn around the spindle until mostly wound up but still long enough to pull up and hook on the hook.
Fan the end of the yarn out and lay a new rolag or piece of fleece onto the existing yarn. Roll the spindle and continue pinching and drafting.

Heavy Cardboard-8 ½"x4"
Scissors
Warp yarn- worsted weight cotton works well
Weft Yarn- wool or cotton
Yarn Needle
Button
Needle
Thread

Loom:
       1) Cut a piece of heavy cardboard (not corrugated) 8 1/2" x 4"
       2) Make 1/4" deep cuts 1/4" apart across both 4" ends of the cardboard
       3) Fold the cardboard 3" from the top leaving 5 1/2" on the other side

Warping:
       4) Catch worsted weight Cotton or warp yarn in the first notch on the 3" side
       5) Bring the yarn around the fold in the cardboard and into the notch behind the cardboard; and back through the next notch
       6) Repeat across alternating front and back
       7) Tie or tape the end to secure

Weaving:
       8) Leaving a 3" tail, begin weaving over and under across one side at the folded edge of the cardboard
       9) When the edge is reached continue around to the other side
       10) Continue weaving first one side then turning the loom and weaving the other side
       11) To change colors or add a new strand, leave an end 3" long of the old strand and 3" long of the new strand and continue weaving. Alternatively, overlap old and new yarns and continue weaving.
       12) Pack the weft tightly
       13) When top of the 3" side is reached, weave back and forth only on the longer flap of the 5 1/2" side

Finishing:
       14) Sew in all yarn ends with a yarn needle
       15) Slip warps off of the cardboard
       16) Sew the button onto the body of the bag
       17) Sew a loop onto the flap

Loading the hand cards

Carding the fleece

Doffing the fleece

Spindle

Spinning

Weaving

Weaving

Fourth Grade Verses

Opening:

The sheep have given us their wool,
The plants their colors bright,
And we have shaped needles out of wood
For us to knit by golden light.
Our fingers that knit and do crochet
Can sew a seed and cut the hay.
They cast a seam and sew a stitch.
They hammer and nail and dig a ditch.
They can create an object of worth,
Of wonder, of beauty, of color, or mirth.
So let us go to work right now
And sew and stitch, both me and thou.

Closing:

My work for now is over,
My hands for now must rest.
I thank you hands,
Both right and left,
For helping me to do my best.

Alternate opening:

My two arms are folded so straight on my chest
Crossing each other with right over left;
I think of the trees crossing branches and twigs,
Vines in the forest, legs dancing a jig;
Windowpanes, rafters and joists in the floor,
Soldiers at battle cross-bright flashing swords;
When crossing the street or crossing my T's,
Birds fly above me, worms crawl under my feet,
Each cross-stitch I do is so perfect and true,
A mirror of the world in all that I do

Lesson Plan for Handwork

Grade four:
THE GOALS FOR THIS YEAR ARE:
- To learn and become proficient with several basic hand sewing stitches
- To learn to use a thimble
- To have an experience of how design and color can be used to show balance, symmetry, and a gesture of openness, through the use of embroidery and cross-stitch
- To have an experience of the reaffirming and grounding affects of cross-stitch
- To be able to take their work home and remember to bring it back on handwork days
- To strengthen and make the hands more capable
- To find completion in all work by considering time management and organization of materials
- To continue to foster a joy for work and a feeling for beauty and color

THE MAIN SKILLS TO BE INTRODUCED AND FURTHER DEVELOPED THIS YEAR ARE:
- Basic hand sewing stitches-running stitch, backstitch, blind hemstitch, chain stitch, buttonhole stitch, blanket stitch, tailor's knot and other decorative stitches as needed
- To continue the use of the thimble
- Butterfly stitch
- Cross-stitch

TIME LINE OF PROJECTS: (Class is held 2 times a week for 50 minutes each)
August-September 15
- Introduction to chain stitch-Spiral Bean Bag

September 15-November
- Handwork bag-design
- Transfer pattern
- Chain-stitch embroidery

December-January
- Folded Paper Stars
- Sew bag together
- Buttonhole stitch loops
- Butterfly stitch cord

February-June
- Cross-stitch Treasure bag
- Cross-stitch Pin Cushion
- Cross-stitch Fountain Pen Case

Upon entering fourth grade, the student leaves behind the world of oneness and becomes aware of his or her own separateness and individuality. They look back on their parents, siblings and teachers as if from a distance, separate from themselves. With their new separateness comes an ability to look at the world and reflect upon it. They are ready for more responsibility and are confident in themselves as individuals. With the study of man and animal, they learn what it is to be human and that in human hands and feet we experience our capacity for human freedom. Hands can do deeds of love and serve both human beings and animals. We need to bring the world to the fourth grader in a way that everywhere expresses its human meaning. By presenting our materials with care, we can show them a world of beauty and goodness.

The fourth grade main lesson curriculum introduces overlapping forms that braid and weave together. A new style of form drawing is introduced that shows the three-dimensionality and layers of the form drawing. In the handwork curriculum, the projects center on cloth. The hemp summer cloth used for the handwork bags has an easily discernable weave. The Aida cloth used for cross-stitch has an even easier to see under and over weave. The crossing of the warp and weft strengthens the newly forming sense of independence that began with the 9-year-change and continues to develop. The cross symbolizes the balance of the heavenly influences pushing in or down and the earthly influences pushing up and out.

Chain Stitch Bean Bag

Hemp summer cloth #64 – 2 -4" square pieces
Perle cotton #5: 1- 36" length each: Red, Orange, Yellow, Green, Blue, & Purple
Chenille Needle # 18
Pencil
White thread
Beans or rice

With a pencil, draw a 3" square centered on 1 piece of the hemp summer cloth. Then draw a spiral filling the space in the center of the 3" square.

Thread the needle with the blue thread. Pull the thread until one end is longer than the other. Knot the thread. Pull the thread through from the wrong side of the fabric along the 3"square pencil line. Sew along the square with a running stitch, about ¼" per stitch. Next, continuing with the blue thread, sew along the spiral with a chain stitch. When the blue thread runs out, knot and change to purple thread. Continue sewing along the spiral. When you reach the center of the spiral, sew over the end of the thread, turn and sew back along the side of the spiral. Continue sewing around the spiral moving through the colors in rainbow order.

Lay the 2 pieces of hemp right sides together. Sew ½" from the edge with backstitch around 3 ½ sides, knot the thread. Leave an opening for turning. Turn right side out. Fill with rice or beans. Sew up the opening.

Hemp summer cloth #64 – 34"x 15" piece
Perle cotton, #5: cut into 36" lengths: 2 color families; could include several shades of each
Chenille Needle #18
Graphite Pencil
Drawing Paper, cut to 12"x 15"
Fabric Pen
White sewing thread
Sewing needle
Yellow pencil
Cotton worsted weight yarn in the same 2 colors as the Perle Cotton

On the paper, draw a design for the handwork bag that includes the ideas: 1) open at the top 2) bilateral symmetry; 3) non-representational; 4) and having a holding quality. The drawing should fill the paper. The design should be open at the top indicating on which side the opening of the bag will be and closed at the bottom of the bag. When you are satisfied with the design, go over it several times with the graphite pencil. Fold the Hemp summer cloth in half, creating two 14" x 15" sides, crease the fold. Slip the design between the layers of the fabric and check whether the design can be seen through the fabric well enough to trace. Make sure the open end of the design aligns with the narrow open end of the fabric and the bottom edge of the paper is close to the fold, (the top 2" of the fabric will be turned inside to finish the bag.) Trace the design with the fabric pen.

Embroidering the design:
Choose 2 color families to work with. There can be many shades of each color but only 2 colors. Pick one color and begin embroidering with chain stitch. Make sure that the colors are used symmetrically on each side of the design.
Once all the lines have been embroidered, go back and embroider another line of stitching close to the first line of stitching and shadowing the original embroidery. When all the lines have been embroidered and re-embroidered, design a monogram to embroider in the lower center of the design. Try to make it symmetrical also. Once you have a design you are happy with, trace it onto the fabric and embroider it with chain stitch.
A third color may be added as a sparkle of color.

Sewing the bag:
Fold the bag in half lengthwise so the embroidery is facing up and all the edges match up. Pin the two side edges of the bag together. Leave the top open. Pin the sides in 3 places and draw a seam line with yellow colored pencil ½" from the edge. Sew along the seam line with white thread using a small, tight backstitch. Sew both sides.

Turn the bag inside out and press the seams with an iron. Pin the sides in 3 places and mark a sewing line with the yellow pencil ½" from the edge or outside of the previous seam allowance. Sew along the seam line with white thread using a small, tight backstitch. Sew both sides.

Hem at opening: Fold over 1/2" along the opening of the bag and press with a hot iron. Fold over again 1 ½"; press with a hot iron. Sew along the first folded edge with invisible hemstitch.

Loops:
Preparation:
With the bag inside out, mark 5 places on each side along the hem as follows: Measure 1" from the side edge, make a dot with the graphite pencil on the inside of the hem ¼" from the bottom of the Hem. Make another dot 1/4" from the top of the bag. Continue making pairs of dots 2 ½" apart across the hem of the bag. 5 pairs of dots per side, 10 total.

Sewing Loops:
With Perle cotton and a color already used on the bag, come up between the layers of fabric and out at a lower dot. Make 3 small stitches in one place, only going through 1 layer of the fabric. Sew through to the outside of the bag at the lower dot; make a stitch to the upper dot going through all layers of fabric. Come back out next to the last stitch and make another long stitch very close to the first stitch. Go through all the layers of fabric. Come back out to the right side of the fabric close to the last stitch and begin the buttonhole stitch around the 2 long stitches. Work buttonhole stitch along the entire length of the 2 stitches. Sew to the inside of the bag and make 3 small stitches to knot the thread. Sew inside of the layers of fabric and come out to the outside of the bag. Trim thread.
Make 10 loops.

Cord:
With the cotton yarn, butterfly stitch a cord four times as long as the top of the bag. Another way to say it: long enough to go twice around the bag plus a little more. Finish off the cord. Cut the cord in half and thread one half through the loops from the right side of the bag, tie the ends together. Thread the other half of the cord through the loops from the left side of the bag, tie the ends together.

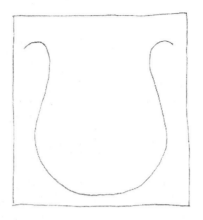

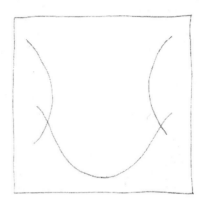

open, symetrical, non-representational
designs

Butterfly Stitch
  * start with a slip knot

* pull color 2 through
  the color 1 loop

*Pull color 1 through
color 2 loop

*Alternate
colors 1 & 2

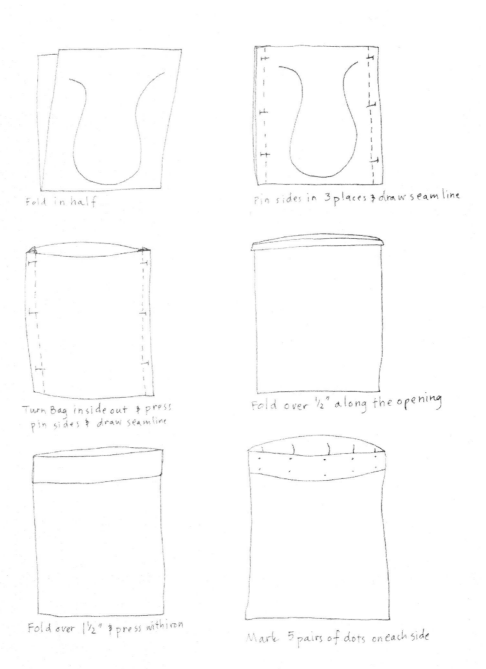

Fold in half

Pin sides in 3 places & draw seam line

Turn Bag inside out & press
pin sides & draw seamline

Fold over ½" along the opening

Fold over 1½" & press with iron

Mark 5 pairs of dots on each side

Cross-stitch has rules:

1.) Each cross-stitch is completed before moving on:
> *Lower left to upper right,*
> *Upper left to lower right.*

2.) Work proceeds to the left up or down.

3.) The work has two ends, the top and bottom and two sides, right and left; the stitches are always made with the one of the ends facing you, either end is okay. Stitches are not made with the sides facing you.

To begin a project:

1.) Measure a piece of Erda cloth to the desired size then add an extra border of 3 rows of holes on all sides. Cut out.

2.) To protect the cloth as it is stitched: using Perle cotton, sew around the cloth with blanket stitch. Begin each stitch 3 holes in from the edge. A blanket stitch can be worked in each hole or every other hole around.

3.) Using the sewing thread, sew a row of running stitches down the middle row of the Erda cloth either through the holes or through the middle of the squares. Make 2 rows of stitching: one running across from side to side and one running up and down.

Beginning and ending cross-stitch thread or yarn:

1.) To begin, pull the thread or yarn through the desired hole until there is 1" of yarn or thread at the back of the work. Work the cross-stitches.

2.) To end: Pull the thread or yarn to the back of the work, sew under 5 stitches. Cut the thread or yarn close to where it exits the last stitch.

To finish the work:

1.) If using fabric:
> a) cut a piece of fabric the same size as the Erda cloth.
> b) Place the cross-stitch piece and the fabric together with right sides facing.
> c) Pin in place.
> d) Sew with a tight backstitch in the first row of cross-stitches leaving a space several inches long to turn.
> e) Turn right side out.
> f) Push the corners out gently with the closed point of a pair of scissors.
> g) Fold the fabric and cross-stitch in neatly at the opening and sew the edges together with zipper stitch.

2.) For felt:
> a) Cut a piece of felt the same size as the cross-stitch stitching (exclude the blanket stitch edge.
> b) Fold the edges of the cross-stitch under and press with a hot iron to crease.

c) Lay the felt onto the back of the cross-stitch. Using thread that matches the felt, sew the felt and cross-stitch together using either a blanket stitch or whipstitch.

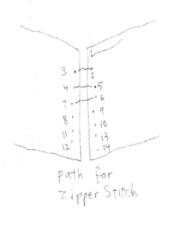

path for
Zipper Stitch

path for
Cross-stitch

3" x 3" piece of Erda cloth, 7 holes to the inch
Perle cotton
Tapestry needle #16
Tapestry wool, several shades both light and dark
Felt for backing
Chenille needle
Perle cotton
Cotton yarn in colors to match tapestry wool

Finish edges on the 3" x 3" square of Erda cloth (see Cross stitch overview)

Mark the center of the cloth by sewing a line of stitching across from the center of each side

Beginning in the center, work a 3 x 3 or 4 x4 stitch square in a light color. Sew the yarn end in and choose a new color.

Work concentric squares around the first square always stitching from right to left or up and down.

Fill up the entire 2" x 2" space inside of the edge stitching.

Fold under the unstitched edge of the Erda cloth all the way around. Press with an iron. A steam cloth might help. Cut 2 pieces of felt the same size as the finished project, about 2" x 2".

Use the Perle cotton and a whipstitch to sew one piece of the felt to the first row of the cross-stitch on each side.

Sew the second piece of felt to the felt on 3 sides. Leave one side open to create the pocket.

Finger knit a cord long enough to go around your neck, about 26". I tell my students to make it reach across their desks. Make a knot in one end of the cord; pull it through a space in the stitching between the 2 pieces of felt close to the top of the bag. Thread the cord onto the tapestry needle; pull it through the stitching on the opposite side of the opening from the inside of the bag between the layers of felt. Make an overhand knot and trim the ends.

5" x 5" piece of Erda cloth, 7 holes to the inch
Perle cotton
Tapestry needle #16
Tapestry wool, several shades both light and dark
Fabric for backing, velveteen works well
Sewing pins
Chenille needle
Perle cotton
Fleece for stuffing

Finish the edges on the 5" x 5" square of Erda cloth (see Cross stitch overview.)

Mark the center of the Erda cloth by sewing across from the center of each side and the diagonals from corner to corner.

Beginning in the center, work a 4x4 stitch square in a light color. Sew yarn end in and choose another light color.

Work a cross out from the center of each side, 2 stitches wide and 6 stitches high; the cross is 4 stitches wide and 2 high.

Fill in the corners with a medium color. Continue adding stitches so that the shapes and colors are symmetrical.

See chart for ideas.

Cut a 5" x 5" piece of fabric (the same size as the Erda cloth.) Place the cross-stitch piece and fabric together with right sides facing. Pin in place. Sew with a tight backstitch in the first row of cross-stitches around 3 ½ sides leaving a space several inches long to turn. Turn right side out. Push the corners out gently with the closed point of a pair of scissors. Stuff the pincushion firmly with fleece. Fold the fabric and cross-stitch edges to the inside of the pincushion and sew the opening together with whipstitch.

Chart for Pin Cushion

Watercolor Paper, cut into 4" x 9" pieces
Watercolor paints
Watercolor paintbrush
5" x 20" piece of Erda cloth, 7 holes to the inch
Perle cotton
Tapestry needle #16
Tapestry wool, several shades both light and dark
Fabric for backing, cotton fabric works well
Chenille needle
Perle cotton
Sewing thread
Sewing pins
Chalk
Button

To create the design:
Fold the watercolor paper in half lengthwise. Open the paper out. Paint with the watercolor paints. Fold in half to make a mirror image, press and open out. Try several designs.

Preparing the Erda cloth:
Finish the edges on the 5" x 20" piece of Erda cloth (see Cross stitch overview)

Sew across the Erda cloth 4 ½" from one end and 6 ½" from the other.

Count across the 5" side of the cloth to find the center either a row of holes or between the rows of holes. Sew a running stitch the length of the cross-stitch fabric marking the center.

Cross-stitch design:
Beginning with the 5" x 9" rectangle in the center, stitch the design from the watercolor onto the fabric. Choose one half of the watercolor to follow and copy that design onto both halves of the cross-stitch fabric.

Next mirror the design onto the smaller rectangles.

Finishing:
Cut a 5" x 20" piece of fabric (the same size as the Erda cloth.) Place the cross-stitch piece and fabric together with right sides facing. Pin in place. Sew with a tight backstitch in the first row of cross-stitches around 3 ½ sides leaving a space several inches long to turn. Turn right side out. Push the corners out gently with the closed point of a pair of scissors. Fold the fabric edge and the cross-stitch edge to the inside and sew the opening closed with zipper stitch.

Fold the 6 ½" rectangle up to the larger rectangle, wrong sides together. Sew along the side edges with blanket stitch to create a pocket; leave the top edge open.

Button loop and button:

With Perle cotton, pull thread from the inside at the end of the flap, ½" from the center. Make 3 small stitches to secure the thread. Take a stitch over your finger, coming out 1/2" from the center of the flap. Sew around the loop with a buttonhole stitch. Secure the thread and sew in the end. Place the fountain pen into the pocket and fold over the top flap. With the chalk, make a mark through the loop for the button placement. Sew the button onto the pocket.

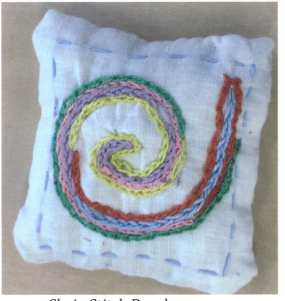

Chain Stitch Beanbag

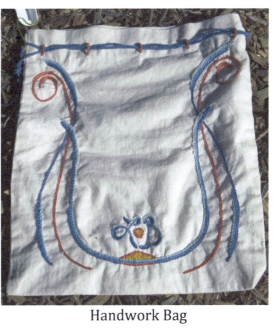

Handwork Bag

Treasure Bag

Pincushion

Fountain Pen Case

Opening:
May I do my work with patience,
May I do my work with care,
May my fingers work as friends together,
And I my laughter share.

Closing:
I've done my work with patience,
I've done my work with care,
My fingers have worked as friends together,
And I my laughter shared.

Lesson Plan for Handwork

Grade five:
THE GOALS FOR THIS YEAR ARE:

-To build upon an already established foundation in knitting introducing new elements that prepare for 3-dimensional planning, thinking and imagining

-To be able to knit, purl and decrease, rib and cable

- To be able to use 4 needles to knit in the round

-To be able to correct mistakes

-To foster logical thinking in being able to read instructions, follow them, and write their own

-To continue to foster a sense of responsibility by being able to take work home and bring it back on handwork days

-To be able to help others

-To strengthen and make the hands more capable

-To continue to foster a joy for work and a feeling for beauty and color

-To complete a hat

THE MAIN SKILLS TO BE INTRODUCED AND FURTHER DEVELOPED THIS YEAR ARE:

-To learn the process of paste paper

-To learn pamphlet stitch

-To learn and become proficient at knitting

-To learn to read knitting patterns

-To be able to read and understand written instructions

-To learn to sew in ends and finish a knitting project

-To learn proper yarn management-ball rolling and skein tying

-Staying organized

TIME LINE OF PROJECTS: (Class is held 2 times a week for 50 minutes each)

August

Handwork Book

September 1-September 15

-Write knitting terms

-Shape and sand knitting needles

-Write knitting instructions for hat

September 15-December

-Hatband

-Folded Paper Star

January

-Hat- Crown

February

-Fingerless Mitts

March-June

-Socks

-Cabled Headband

-Cabled Hat

-Yoga Socks

The students enter fifth grade with a new and different feeling. They are steadier and more self-confident. They have become accustomed to being an isolated self and are ready to step across a new threshold. The fifth grader is at a more balanced stage of development and has a need for harmony. They are beginning to stand more firmly on the ground. Their bodies are coming down to Earth while their minds reach up into the heavens. The feelings for the fifth grade are: "Through strength, through ability, I am here"; and "I can do with will." They are ready to take on the journey through human consciousness. The study of the evolution of human consciousness supports them where they are. Ancient History brings them into themselves through an education of the feelings. They learn what it is to be human and begin shifting from a dreamlike consciousness to waking consciousness, just as the ancient Persians began to use the Earth with agriculture. As a balance to the inwardness of ancient history, geography leads them away from themselves, from the familiar to the unfamiliar.

As teachers, we must change our attitude in the classroom and step up to becoming a teacher respected by older children. The fifth grade student is beginning to own their own work, to make decisions and be freer and less formed. They respond to a practical, productive and creative working environment. It is time for them to wake up and focus. We can allow them to learn from each other, so some talking is allowed in class. We can also allow them to struggle in their learning. They are learning to read and write instructions, how to organize their time and projects and how to give instruction to one another. They need projects that function in their lives, useful projects using natural materials. The projects should take a long time so that they can struggle through the eye of the needle and triumph. Goals need to be set and met. Handwork develops strength by making them use their hands.

This year marks a change in the handwork process; students write out their own directions in their handwork books.

Finished size 9" x 6"

> Cover: 1 piece of Cardstock- 12" x 9"
> Pages: 10 pages 8 ½" x 11" printer paper
> Rice flour
> Water
> Small saucepan
> Green Tempura or Acrylic paint
> Newspaper or scrap paper
> Perle cotton or heavy thread/ weaving warp cut into 36" lengths
> Chenille needle

Paste paper cover:

 Mix ½ cup rice flour with ½ cup water. Stir until smooth. Bring 3 cups of water to a boil and pour into the rice flour. Stir constantly until thoroughly mixed. Add the paint a little bit at a time until the desired color is reached. Allow the paste to cool. Place the cover paper on a surface protected with newspaper or scrap paper. Spread 2 tablespoons of the rice paste evenly onto the cover paper. Add more rice paste until the paper surface is thinly covered. Use fingers, paint spatulas etc., to make designs on the cover. Designs can be reworked until a satisfactory design is achieved. When you are satisfied with the design, allow the cover to dry.

Sewing the cover:

Fold the sheets of printer paper in half one at a time. Open out one sheet and layer one sheet on top of another sheet. Refold the paper as a group. Fold the cover in half and crease. Place the folded pages into the cover aligning the folds. Thread the needle with the Perle cotton or warp thread. Starting from the inside of the book, go through all the layers of the pages and the cover at the midpoint. Pull the thread through until a 4" tail remains. Go back through all layers ¼ of the way from the top, the thread is now inside the book. Go back to the outside of the book ¼ of the way from the bottom of the book, thread is now on the outside of the book. Sew back through the midpoint, the first hole. Arrange the tail of the thread on one side of the center thread and the needle and thread on the other side, tie a double knot. Trim the ends. The cover may be trimmed if it extends too far beyond the pages.

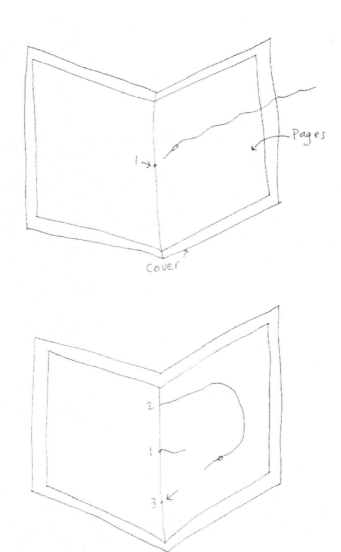

4-9" long 4mm diameter hardwood dowels
100-grit sandpaper
220-grit sandpaper
Beeswax
Rag for buffing
Sharpie marker

Write the student's name in the middle of each dowel. Sand both ends of each dowel into a tapered point with the 100-grit sandpaper. Support the dowel with your index finger while sanding. Make sure the point is long and gradually tapers to a gentle point. Sand the entire needle with the 220-sandpaper until it is as smooth as silk. Coat the sanded needle all over with beeswax. Use the rag to buff the needle until it is smooth. Repeat for the remaining dowels.

Materials: worsted weight yarn in one or several colors
Knitting Needles: 4-size 6 Double-pointed needles
Yarn needle
Crochet Hook size H
Stitch Markers

Band:
With straight needles, cast on 10 stitches, knit until piece measures 19" and/or fits around the head. Bind off. Do not cut the yarn

Using the crochet hook and yarn, pick up one stitch for each garter stitch ridge across one long edge of the band, place the stitches onto a knitting needle. It may take more than one needle to accommodate all the stitches.

Count the stitches and divide by three. With the first double pointed needle (needle #1), knit 1/3 of the stitches; with the second needle (needle #2), knit 1/3 of the stitches; with the third needle (needle #3), knit the remaining stitches.

Form the needles into a triangle. Using the yarn needle, sew the bind off edge of the hatband to the cast on edge of the hatband with whipstitch, fasten off the yarn with 3 small stitches and sew in the yarn end. Hatband created.

Crown:
With an empty needle, begin knitting stitches from needle #1 and continue onto needles 2 and 3 as you go around. One row completed.

Continue knitting around from needle to needle until the hat is 7" tall overall.

Count the stitches and divide by 8, this equals x. Count the stitches and place a marker after every x number of stitches.

Decrease round:
Knit 2 stitches together, knit to marker, slide marker, knit 2 stitches together.

Continue around to beginning of the round; decrease at the beginning of each needle and after each marker; 8 stitches decreased

Plain round: Knit

Alternate between decrease rounds and plain rounds until 8 stitches remain. Break the yarn 8" from the work; thread the yarn onto the needle, and run it through the remaining 8 stitches. Pull tightly and thread the yarn end to the inside of the hat. Sew all ends in.

Materials: Worsted weight yarn
Knitting Needles: 4-size 6 double-pointed needles
Yarn needle

Cuff:
Cast 36 Stitches onto one needle.

With a second needle, work knit 2 Purl 2 rib over 12 stitches
With a third needle, work knit 2 Purl 2 rib over 12 stitches
With a fourth needle, work knit 2 Purl 2 rib over 12 stitches

Form the three needles into a triangle; the first stitch on needle 1 next to the last stitch on needle 3; examine the stitches carefully to see if there are any twists in the stitches. Begin to work in the round: with the extra needle work the stitches on needle 1; continuing in knit 2 purl 2 ribbing for 1".

Change to stockinette stitch-knit every row. Keep knitting until the work measures 4" from the cast on edge. End with the third needle of a round.

Thumb:
Knit 4 stitches, Cast off 6 stitches. Finish knitting the round.

Next round:
Knit 4 stitches, cast on 6 stitches. Finish knitting the round. Continue in stockinette stitch until the work measures 6"

Next round begin Knit 2 Purl 2 ribbing. Continue until work measures 7".

Cast off. Sew in all yarn ends with a yarn needle.

Repeat for second Hand warmer.

Materials: Worsted weight yarn
Knitting Needles: 4-size 6 double pointed needles
Yarn needle

Cuff:
Cast 40 Stitches onto one needle.

With a second needle, work knit 2 purl 2 ribbing over 12 stitches
With a third needle, work knit 2 purl 2 ribbing over 16 stitches
With a fourth needle, work knit 2 purl 2 ribbing over 12 stitches

Form the three needles into a triangle, the first stitch on needle 1 next to the last stitch on needle 3, examine the stitches to see if there are any twists in the stitches. Begin to work in the round: with needle 4 work the stitches on needle 1; continuing in knit 2 purl 2 ribbing.

Continue to work the next needle to the left with the empty needle; 3 needles equal one round. Work round and round in ribbing until the work measures 1". Change to stockinette stitch- knit every round. Knit until the work measures 4" from the cast on edge. End with the third needle of a round.

Heel Flap:
Arrange the stitches so that needle 1 has 20 stitches and needle 2 has 20 stitches.

Row 1: Working only with the stitches on needle 1 and with the right side facing, with an empty needle: slip 1, knit 1, across the row. At the end of the 20 stitches, turn work.

Row 2: Slip 1, purl to the end of the row. Turn work.
Repeat rows 1 and 2 until the heel flap measures 2 ½"; end with a purl row.

Heel turn:
Row 1: Knit 10 stitches, place marker. Knit 1, knit 2 together, knit 1. Turn work.

Row 2: purl to marker, slip marker, purl 1, purl 2 together, purl 1. Turn work.

Row 3: Knit to 1 stitch before the gap created by the last turn, knit 2 together, knit 1. Turn work.

Row 4: Purl to 1 stitch before the gap created by the last turn, purl 2 together, purl 1. Turn work.

Repeat rows 3 and 4 until there are 12 stitches left on the needle; end with a purl row.

Gusset:

With needle 1, knit across the 12 heel stitches, pick up 12 stitches along the side of the heel flap. With needle 2, knit across the 20 stitches that have been waiting on a separate needle. With needle 3, pick up 12 stitches on the other side of the heel flap; knit 6 stitches from needle 1. Needle 1 now has 18 stitches; needle 2 has 20 stitches; and needle 3 has 18 stitches.

Round 1: Begin knitting on needle 1, knit to the last 3 stitches, knit 2 together, knit 1. Knit across needle 2; with needle 3, knit 1, knit 2 together, knit to the end of the round.

Round 2: Knit one round plain.
Repeat rounds 1 and 2 until there are 40 stitches left

Foot:

Knit until the sock reaches to your little toe when it is tried on.

Toe:

Round 1: Needle 1: Knit to the last 3 stitches, knit 2 together, knit 1;
Needle 2: knit 1, knit 2 together, knit to the last 3 stitches, knit 2 together, knit 1;
Needle 3: knit 1, knit 2 together, knit to the end of the needle.

Round 2: Knit one round plain.

Repeat rounds 1 and 2 until 8 stitches are left.
Arrange stitches onto 2 needles so that there are 4 stitches on each needle.
Break the yarn 18" from the work and thread onto the yarn needle.

Kitchener Stitch: Hold the needles so they are parallel to each other and horizontal to the ground, with the yarn needle go into the first stitch on the front needle as if to knit, slide the stitch off the knitting needle onto the yarn needle, go into the next stitch on the front needle as if to purl, pull the yarn through the stitch but leave it on the knitting needle. Go into the first stitch on the back needle as if to purl and slide it off the knitting needle onto the yarn needle; go into the next stitch on the back needle as if to knit, pull the yarn through the stitch but leave it on the knitting needle.

Repeat the Kitchener Stitch across the needles. Pull the yarn through the final stitches. Sew in all yarn ends.

Repeat for the second sock

Worsted Weight yarn
Knitting needles: 4-Size 6 double pointed
Yarn Needle
Crochet Hook Size H
5 stitch markers

Cable Band:
Cast 18 stitches onto one needle. Work back and forth on two needles as follows:
   Row 1- Knit 4, Purl 2, Knit 6, Purl 2, Knit 4
   Row 2- Knit 6, Purl 6, Knit 6

Repeat rows 1 and 2, 5 more times, 12 rows total, end with row 2

Cable row-Knit 4, Purl 2, slip 3 stitches onto a cable needle and place in the back of the work, knit 3, knit 3 from the cable needle, Purl 2 Knit 4

Repeat row 2

Repeat the above 14 rows until the knitted band fits around the head, between 18-22", cast of
Sew the ends together

Materials: Worsted weight yarn
Knitting Needles: 4-size 6 double pointed needles
Yarn needle

Cuff:
Cast 40 Stitches onto one needle.

With a second needle, work knit 2 Purl 2 ribbing over 12 stitches
With a third needle, work knit 2 Purl 2 ribbing over 16 stitches
With a fourth needle, work knit 2 Purl 2 ribbing over 12 stitches

Form the three needles into a triangle, the first stitch on needle 1 next to the last stitch on needle 3, examine the stitches to see if there are any twists in the stitches. Begin to work in the round; continuing in knit 2 purl 2 ribbing for 1".

Change to stockinette stitch- knit every row. Continue until the work measures 5 1/2" from the cast on edge. End with the third needle of a round.

Heel:
Cast off 18 stitches. Knit the remaining stitches in the round.

At the beginning of the next round, cast on 18 stitches. Knit the remaining stitches in the round.

Foot:
Knit until the sock measures 2" past the heel cast on.

Work in Knit 2 purl 2 ribbing for 1"

Cast off.

Sew in all yarn ends

With a matching or contrasting color, blanket stitch around the heel opening.

Make 2.

5th Grade book

Hat

Hand warmers

Socks

Head Band

Opening verse

Within there lies an image
Of all that I can be.
Until I have become it,
I never shall be free.

Closing Verse

Steadfast I stand in the world.
With certainty I tread the path of life.
Love shall be in the depths of my being,
Hope shall be in all deeds,
Confidence I shall impress into my thinking.

Lesson Plan for Handwork

Grade six:
THE GOALS FOR THIS YEAR ARE:

-To familiarize students with working in 3-dimensional space using clay, fabric and wool

-To broaden their sewing ability from flat to a 3-dimensional object

- To develop the ability to keep a record of the process of creating in their handwork books

-To foster the development of a stronger sense of self and a more independent relationship to the world around them

-To support the development of the ability to form abstract concepts

-To awaken the intellect through the will

THE MAIN SKILLS TO BE INTRODUCED AND FURTHER DEVELOPED THIS YEAR ARE:

-To develop the process of paste paper

-To reinforce the pamphlet stitch

-To learn to work with clay in 3-dimensional forms

-To learn to visualize a 2-dimensional drawing in a 3-dimensional form

-To learn to draw a pattern from a drawing

-To continue to build on previously introduced sewing skills

-To learn to take the time to properly stuff and finish a project

-To learn the process of wet felting an article of clothing

TIME LINE OF PROJECTS: (Class is held 2 times a week for 50 minutes each)

August

Handwork Book

September 1-September 15

-Clay Modeling-Sphere, Cube, Pinch pot and Animal

September 15-September 30

-Elephant

-Draw Elephant

-Make pattern

-Seam Allowance

-Cut out fabric

-Extra projects- Needle case, Pencil case, 9-patch bag

October-March

-Sewing the Elephant

-Stuffing the Elephant

-Finishing the Elephant

April-

-Dye wool for Slippers

-Card wool for Slippers

-Felted Slippers

May-June

-Coat of Arms

With sixth grade, the student enters a new level of development, pre-adolescence. They are leaving childhood behind and entering the world of adult thinking consciousness. As they grow, the students are developing a stronger sense of self and a more independent relationship to the world around them. Inwardly a new depth of feeling is developing and as the astral body awakens much turmoil arises in their souls. The imaginative thinking of the child metamorphoses to the ability to form abstract concepts. The character of thought changes to a more conceptual nature that will develop into the full-blown power of the human spirit. Physically, children grow angular and lanky. Their movements become awkward as if they no longer fit into their bodies. As they separate from the world of childhood, they are pulled down into the Earth's forces of gravity. It is the job of the handwork curriculum to awaken the intellect through the will. As they come into the earth and become aware of the sense of other, the projects must ask them to be more exact. The saying "clumsy fingers point to a clumsy intellect" reinforces the fact that manual work develops the intellect. Intelligence is formed through movement and manual dexterity. Handwork is done in order to develop the capacities of the students.

6th grade book: finished size 9" x 7"
      Cover: 1 piece of Cardstock- 14" x 9"
      Pages: 10 pages 8 ½" x 14" printer paper
      ½ cup Rice flour
      3 ½ cups Water
      Small saucepan
      Tempura or Acrylic paint-teal
      Perle cotton or heavy thread/ weaving warp
      Chenille needle

Paste paper cover:

Mix ½ cup rice flour with ½ cup water. Stir until smooth. Bring 3 cups of water to a boil and pour into the rice flour. Stir constantly until thoroughly mixed. Add the paint a little bit at a time until the desired color is reached. Allow the paste to cool. Place cover paper on a surface protected with newspaper or scrap paper. Spread 2 tablespoons of paste evenly onto the cover paper. Add more paste until the paper surface is evenly and thinly covered. Use fingers, paint spatulas etc., to make designs on the cover. Designs can be reworked until a satisfactory design is achieved. When you are satisfied with the design, allow the cover to dry.

Sewing the cover:

Fold the sheets of paper in half one at a time. Open out one sheet and layer one sheet on top of another sheet. Refold the paper as a group. Fold the cover in half and crease. Place the folded pages into the cover aligning the folds. Thread the needle with the Perle cotton or warp thread. Starting from the inside of the book, go through all the layers of the pages and the cover at the midpoint. Pull the thread through until a 4" tail remains. Go back through all layers ¼ of the way from the top; the thread is now inside the book. Go back to the outside of the book ¼ of the way from the bottom of the book; the thread is now on the outside of the book. Sew back through the first hole at the midpoint. Arrange the thread tail on one side of the center thread and the needle and thread on the other side, tie a double knot. Trim the ends. The cover may be trimmed if it extends too far beyond the pages.

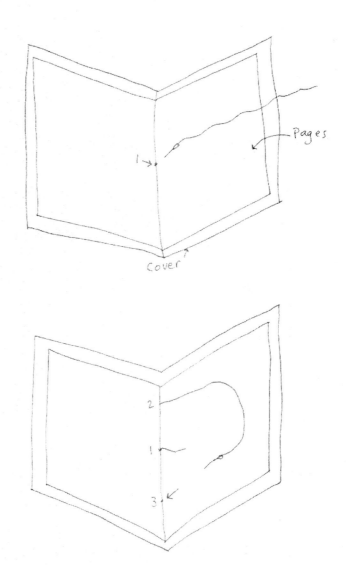

Sphere:
Materials: Orange size piece of clay set on a board or piece of heavy card

Pinch a marble size piece of clay away from the larger piece and roll it into a sphere.

Add quarter size pieces of clay around the original sphere smoothing as you work and maintaining the spherical shape. Continue adding and smoothing, rolling the clay between the palms to shape.

Hold the sphere in the hands.

Do not set it down or roll it on a tabletop or other surface.

When the sphere fits comfortably in the palm with little space to spare the sphere is done.

Have the students stand and form a circle.

Step 1: Hold the sphere in the right hand palm up in front of the solar plexus. Cover the sphere with the left palm.

Step 2: Grasp the sphere with the left hand; swing the left arm and hand holding the sphere to the left. Keep the elbows bent. The right hand swings to the right with palm turned up.

Step 3: Adjacent students pass spheres from left hand to their neighbor's right hand. Return to Step 1. Continue to pass spheres from student to student. Work in silence. Check regularly to make sure everyone still has a sphere.

If all is working well, try it with eyes closed.

Have students return to their seats and take the spheres apart piece by piece the same way they were built up. Return the clay to the bucket and spray with water.

Cube:
Materials: Orange size piece of clay set on a board or piece of heavy card

Build a sphere as above.

Once the sphere is made, begin pressing on opposite sides, above/ below, side/side and front/back.

Continue to press gently to form a cube.
After a few minutes, edges will become more apparent.

Continue to hold the cube in your hand, resist the urge to press the cube onto a tabletop to flatten.

The best result will come from continuing to press the sphere between the palms.

When 10 minutes are left in the class time, have the students place the cubes all onto one table.

Look at all the cubes. Admire them. Compare how flat the surfaces are, how sharp the edges are etc.

Have students return to their seats and take the spheres apart piece by piece the same way they were built up. Return the clay to the bucket and spray with water.

Inside/Outside:
Materials: Orange size piece of clay set on a board or piece of heavy card

Build a sphere as above.

Once spheres are made, begin pressing with the thumb into the center of the sphere.

First, make a small indentation, turn the sphere, press deeper and out, turn the sphere.

Continue pressing and turning the sphere.

Gradually a bowl or pinch pot will form.

Continue pressing out as if the sides of the pot are turning into a flower bud that is opening.

The pot often begins to crack at this point but continue to press, open out, and turn.

Allow the sides to become convex.

An upside down pot will begin to come together.

Try to smooth the sides and pull it into a smaller and smaller pot.

Hold the clay in your hands at all times. Do not set it onto the table to work.

Eventually form the pot into a ball. Press the ball until it is firm and it has returned to its original form.

Take the sphere apart piece by piece the same way it was put together. Return the clay to the bucket and spray with water.

Elephant

Materials: Start with a lump of clay the size of a bread loaf set onto a board or piece of heavy cardboard on a table.

Ask the students to close their eyes and imagine an elephant walking away from them. Imagine the legs like tree trunks, the large solid body, the swaying walk, the ears flapping at the insects in the steamy sunshine. Ask them whether the trunk is raised in triumph or stretched out to pick up leaves to draw them to his mouth. Or is it lowered to suck water up from a stream.

Now ask them to open their eyes and start forming the elephant as it is walking away from them.

Form it from the lump of clay in front of them without lifting it from the table.

Remove the clay from under the belly to form the legs.

Shape by pressing the clay; pull the clay gently to form the ears.

Try to keep working from the back for as long as possible. Turn the board around to work on the head and ears.

When the elephants are finished or 10 minutes before class ends, have students place the elephants onto one table. Look at all the elephants. Admire them.

Compare how large the ears are, how the trunks arch, are the legs thick enough to hold up an elephant?

Take the elephant apart piece by piece. Return the clay to the bucket and spray with water.

3-4 sheets of drawing paper, 24x36
Pencil
Crayon
Wool fabric in grey or tan-18" x 30"
Pins
Tailors chalk or a pencil
Ruler
Shears
Sewing Pins
Contrasting thread
Grey Thread
Needle
8 ½" x 11" piece of paper
Wool fleece
Scrap Paper
Hardboard or thin cardboard, for example the back of drawing pads or empty cereal
        boxes
Black embroidery floss
Embroidery needle

Drawing

Body:
Draw a large oval in the center of the page.

Head:
Draw a smaller oval 1"-2" away from the upper left side of the original oval.

Neck:
Connect the smaller oval to the larger oval with a double bent curve: begin at the top edge of the smaller oval, curve out around the oval follow its contour as it begins to curve in and then continue the curve back out to join to the larger oval in a smooth line (double bent curve.)

Do the same at the lower edge of the small oval.

Legs:
Mark a point about ¼ of the way across the top of the large oval at each end.
Draw an inverted V down from each point past the lower edge of the large oval to the edge of the paper to designate where the legs will be.

Widen the lines below the lower edge of the oval by ½" – 1" on each side.

Smooth out the connections of the body to each leg with a curve. Connect the forward front and back legs together and the other 2 legs together.

Trunk:
Beginning at the lower edge of the small oval draw a double bent curve for the lower edge of the trunk. Is the trunk raised in the air? Is the trunk lowered? Mirror the double bent curve with another line beginning from the top of the small oval. Make the trunk at least 1 ½" -2" wide.

Trace around the outside edge of the elephant

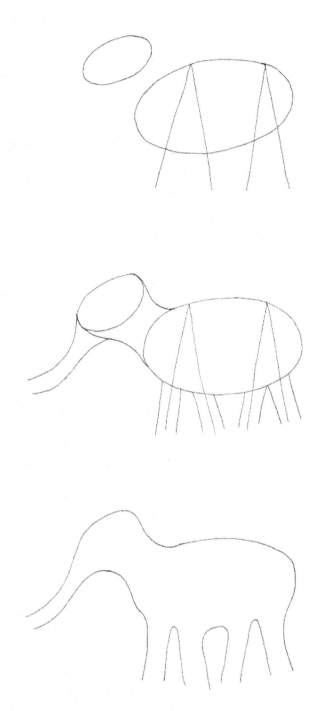

Belly line:
Begin drawing a double bent curve from the chest, dipping above the front legs, rising at the belly, dipping above the back legs and rising towards the tail.

Transfer of the pattern:
Rub the back of the elephant drawing all over with crayon.

Side 1: Place the drawing face up on a clean sheet of paper. Trace around the back, trunk, one front leg and one back leg. Label the drawing "side 1."

Gusset 1: Move the drawing to a clean area of paper. Trace around the same front and back leg and the belly line. Label the drawing "gusset 1."

Rub the back of the elephant drawing with crayon again.

Side 2: Move the drawing to a clean piece of paper. Trace around the back, trunk, the other front and back legs. Label the drawing "side 2."

Gusset 2: Move the drawing to a clean area of paper. Trace around the same front and back leg and the belly line. Label the drawing "gusset 2."

Cut the pattern pieces out. There should be 4 pieces.

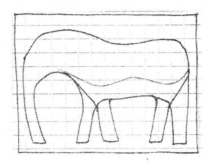

The Belly Line

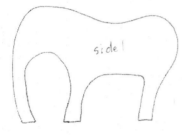

side 1

Gusset 1

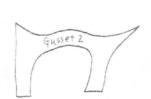

Gusset 2

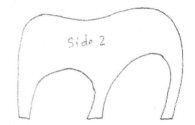

Side 2

Pattern Pieces

Lay the fabric out in a single layer with the selvedge towards the table edge in front of you.

Lay the pattern pieces on the fabric so that side 1 and gusset 1 are facing the same direction. Lay side 2 and gusset 2 facing in the opposite direction from side 1 and gusset 1.

Lay the pattern pieces so there is at least 1" between pattern pieces and at least ½" from the edge of the fabric.

Check to see that the side 1 and side 2 trunks point in opposite directions, one left and one right.

Pin pattern pieces to the fabric. Space the pins about 3" apart and at critical junctures such as curves, trunks and legs.

Using tailors chalk or a pencil, trace around the pattern pieces to mark the sewing line.

Using a ruler and chalk or pencil, mark dots ½" away from the pattern/sewing line. Connect the dots to mark the cutting line.

Check to make sure the elephant sides and their gussets correlate with each other. Have a teacher check the student's work.

Extend the leg lines by ½"-1" and square off the bottom edge.

Cut out the gussets on the cutting line.

Save all scraps!

Leg Gussets

With right sides together, pin the gussets together at the belly line, matching the sewing lines and edges.

Baste with a running stitch and contrasting thread along the belly sewing line.

Mark off the middle 2" of the seam.

Thread the needle with the grey thread. Pull the two ends together and knot. Sew with backstitch. Sew along the belly line from the edge to the middle section; knot the thread. Begin sewing on the other side of the middle 2" along the belly line; knot the thread.

Sewing the Belly Line

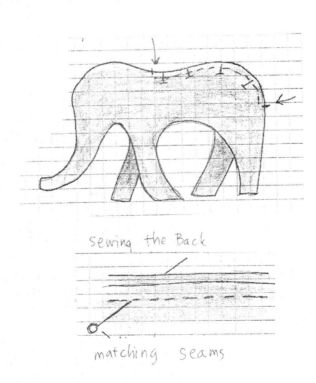

Sewing the Back

matching seams

Cut out side 1.

Pin side 1 to gusset 1, right sides together. Match the sewing lines, the throat and the tail; pin the legs and tummy.

Baste along the legs and tummy with contrasting thread, leaving the bottom of the legs open.

Sew along the legs and tummy with grey thread and a tight backstitch on the sewing lines. Leave the bottom of the legs open, sew all the way to the edge of the fabric.

Repeat with side 2.

Sewing the Back and Trunk

Back:

With right sides together, match the sewing lines along the back of side 1 and side 2. Use a pin to align the sewing lines.

Pin from the tail to the nape of the neck. Do not pin the top of the head.

Baste with contrasting thread along the sewing line from the tail to the nape of the neck.

Sew along the sewing line from the tail to the nape of the neck with a small, tight backstitch and grey thread. Do not sew the top of the head.

Trunk:

Match from the top of the leg gusset to the trunk; leave the end of the trunk open; match the front outer edges of the trunk up to eye level.

Pin from the leg gusset to the tip of the trunk and from the outer edge of the trunk up to eye level.

Baste with contrasting thread along the sewing line from the leg gusset to the tip of the trunk and from the outer edge of the trunk up to eye level.

Sew along the sewing line from the leg gusset to the tip of the trunk and from the outer edge of the trunk up to eye level with a small, tight backstitch and grey thread. Do not sew the top of the head.

Fold the paper in half lengthwise.

Place the folded piece of paper between the two sides of the elephant's head. Slide the paper so that one edge is against the seam on the trunk. The paper should come out of the elephant's head above the eye. Draw a line along the fabric edge from the trunk to the forehead. Press your finger near the top of the elephant's head and pivot the paper to the nape of the elephant's neck. Continue drawing the line along the fabric edge from the forehead to the nape of the elephant's neck.

Remove the paper. Draw an arrow pointing towards the trunk. Cut out the head gusset with the paper folded.

Pin the gusset pattern to the fabric to that the arrow is pointed along the straight of grain. Draw around the edge of the pattern with the chalk or pencil to mark the cutting line.

Cut the gusset out on the cutting line.

Pin the gusset to the head, right sides together. Carefully match the points at the trunk and neck. Baste with contrasting thread along the sewing line from the trunk to the nape of the neck.

Carefully turn the gusset to the right side to check that the proportions look right for the head. Make adjustments if needed.

Turn the head inside out. Sew along the sewing line from the trunk to the nape of the neck with small, tight backstitches and grey thread.

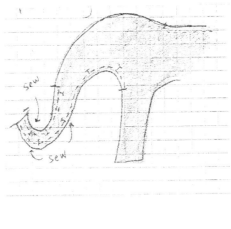

Sewing the trunk

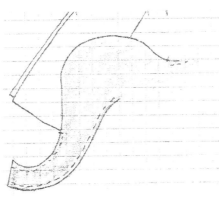

Drawing the head gusset

pivoting the pattern for the head gusset

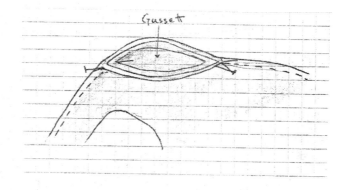

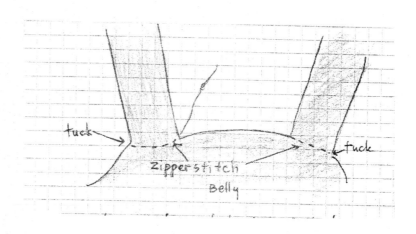

Before turning the elephant right side out, clip the inside and outside curves with the scissors.

Inside curves would include under the belly at the legs and under the trunk.

 Cut almost to the stitching on the seam line. Be careful not to clip the stitching.

Make the clips about ¼" apart.

Outside curves would include the back, the head gussets, and the outside edge of the trunk.

Outside curves are notched. Make small V-shaped cuts around the curve, cutting almost to the stitching.

Wait to trim the seams until the elephant has been turned right side out. The seam allowance may come in handy to enlarge the elephant.

When and if you wish to trim the seam allowance, it is best to trim each layer a different width- for example: ¼" and 3/8".

Carefully turn the animal right side out through the belly opening.

Narrow areas can be turned using the eraser end of a pencil or the point of a closed pair of scissors.

Begin stuffing at the trunk and work back to the shoulder. Make sure to stuff firmly and fill out the shape. Watch the shape of the head form as you stuff it. Is it becoming an elephant?

Continue to stuff the neck until the wrinkles have smoothed out. Once the shoulders are stuffed, begin stuffing the legs. Stuff the legs from both the open foot end and the belly. Stuff very firmly and remember the animal will need to stand up. Hold the leg where you want it to be in relation to the rest of the body and stuff straight down. If the stuffing does not look right, you can always take the stuffing out and re-stuff the leg. The seam line may be adjusted from the outside by using the zipper stitch.

After the legs are stuffed, stuff the body. Take the time to look at your elephant and see if it is coming out as you intended. Adjust the seams in or out with zipper stitch if the shape is not right.

When the elephant is firmly stuffed, try standing the elephant up on its legs. If the legs are not squarely beneath the elephant, they can be adjusted by taking tucks in the "leg pits" with zipper stitch. Begin at the seam line at the top of the leg and make a wedge-shaped tuck. Begin with a very narrow seam and widen the seam as needed. Narrow the seam back to the opposite seam line.

Try standing the elephant up. It may take several tucks to get the animal to stand securely.

The Feet

Check the leg length to see if the legs are different lengths. With chalk or pencil mark all the legs the same length as the shortest leg. Continue the line around the outside of each leg.

Sole Template:
Open out the leg opening and trace around its circumference onto a piece of paper. Make the leg opening as round as possible when drawing the sole template. Correct the shape of the sole template to make it round. Cut out the template and trace around it onto hardboard or cardboard. Cut four feet from the cardboard.

Lay the cutout cardboard foot onto the right side of the fabric. Leaving at least ½" between each foot, trace around the cardboard with a pencil. Draw a ¼" seam allowance around each foot. Cut the feet out on the seam allowance line.

Starting with one round of fabric, sew a running stitch close to the edge of the fabric. Place the cardboard foot on the fabric. Pull the thread tightly to gather the fabric around the foot. Knot securely; do not cut the thread!

Using zipper stitch and a doubled thread, sew the foot onto the bottom of the leg along the level line drawn in the first step above.

Sew until a ½" space remains on the foot seam.

Sew on the 3 remaining feet repeating the same process. When all 4 feet have been attached, check to see if the elephant is level or needs more stuffing to stand correctly. Once any adjustments have been made, sew up the feet seams. Knot securely and tuck in the thread ends.

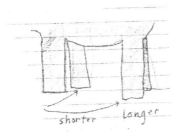

shorter   longer

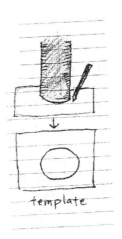

template

Stitch close to edge
of fabric

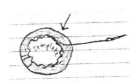

Pull thread to gather

Trunk

Tuck in the seam allowance at the end of the trunk and sew under with invisible stitches so that the elephant can breathe.

Eyes

Mark the position of the eyes with pins. Using embroidery floss, sew through the back of the elephant's head and come out on one side of the eye pin. Sew three long stitches very close together to form the eye. Go back through the head to the side of the other eye pin to sew the second eye with 3 long stitches. Sew back through the head and cut the thread so that it disappears into the head.

Ears

Draw the elephant ears on paper and cut them out. Hold the ears up to the elephant's head to see if the proportions are correct. Once the ear shape and size are correct, lay the paper pattern on two layers of fabric. Trace around the pattern with pencil or chalk to mark the sewing line. Add a ½" seam allowance all around the ear. Cut out the ears. Sew the ears together on the sewing line, right sides together, using matching thread and backstitch. Leave the area next to the head open. Turn the ear right side out. Press the ears into shape. Sew the ear to the head with zipper stitch, tucking in all edges and hiding thread tails.

Tail

Cut a piece of the elephant fabric 1" wide by 3" long and fold into thirds. Hold the tail up to the appropriate place on the elephant to see if the proportions are correct. Zipper stitch the upper third of the tail in place with matching thread. Finish the tail by fringing the lower third of the tail by unraveling the fabric and pulling the threads out.

Wool Felt: Dark Blue - 7" x 4"
              Dark Green – 7" x 4"
              White – 6" x 3 ½"
Perle cotton or embroidery floss in various colors
Chenille needle

Cover:
Front: Fold the dark blue felt in half to make a book cover 3 ½" x 4" on each side. Using a dark color, make small diagonal stitches, about the size of rice grains, across the front cover. Continue making rows of stitches in gradually lighter colors on the cover. Open the cover and notice where your thumb or fingers grip the cover. Leave that space free of embroidery.
Back: Using your choice of Perle cotton, embroider name or initials across the back of the cover.

Lining:
Lay the dark green felt on the wrong side of the cover, match sides and edges. Sew around edge using Perle cotton and blanket stitch. Sew ends to inside

Pages:
Center white felt on green felt. Sew a running stitch down the middle through all the layers. Fold the book in half, using a blanket stitch sew through all layers down the spine of the book.

Sew in all ends.

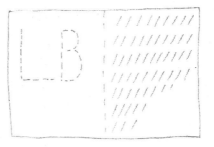

Fold felt in half

Embroider ½

Embroider initials on the other half

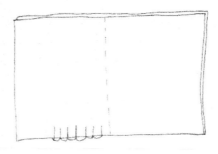

Sew a second piece of felt to the first piece

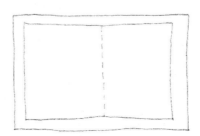

Sew the pages to the cover with running stitch

Sew along the spine with blanket stitch

Upholstery Remnant, 12" x 12" or bigger, edges finished (Felt or other fabric would also work. See Note)
Embroidery Thread or Perle cotton
Chenille Needle

Fold up lower ¼-1/3 of fabric to a form pocket. Whipstitch the folded sides together.

Sew slots for pencils by coming from inside the pocket out to the edge of the pencil slot, either knot thread or sew 3 small stitches in the same place. Sew a straight line of running stitch through both layers of fabric to the top of the pocket. Turn around and sew back in between the previous stitches. Sew across the bottom of the pocket to the next slot seam. Continue across the pocket until at least 6 slots have been created. Knot the thread and sew in all ends.

Finger knit or butterfly stitch a cord about 24" long. Sew onto one side at the top of the pocket.

If using regular fabric: finish the edges with zigzag stitch before starting the Pencil case.

Cotton quilting fabric: ¼ yard light colored fabric

¼ yard dark colored fabric

½ yard lining fabric

¼ yard edging, side and strap fabric

Clear ruler

Tailors Chalk

Shears

Sewing Needle

Thread

Cutting out the Squares:
Straighten the grain of the light colored quilting fabric.

Using the ruler measure 2 ½" from the edge of the long side. Mark with the chalk. Continue to measure and mark in 3 places. Connect the dots by drawing a line with the chalk.

Cut out the strip. Measure 2 ½" from the edge of the strip to make a square; draw a line and cut along the line. Continue to mark and cut squares until you have 10 squares.

Repeat with the dark colored quilting fabric, cutting out 8 squares.

9-patch square:
Arrange the dark and light squares in three rows as follows:

Row 1: *light, dark, light*

Row 2: *dark, light, dark*

Row 3: *light, dark, light*

Row 1: place a light and a dark square right sides together; along one edge sew a ¼" seam with a small tight backstitch, sew three small stitches to finish.Open the squares out and press the seam open with your fingers.

Place a light square onto the opposite edge of the dark square with right sides together. Along the side opposite the first seam, sew a ¼" seam using a small tight back stitch, sew three small stitches to finish.

Sew rows 2 and 3 in the same fashion as row 1, reversing colors for row 2.

Press seams open with an iron.

Place rows 1 and 2 right sides together. Sew one long edge, matching seams. Open the rows out and press the seam open with your fingers. Place row 3 onto the

unsewn edge of row 2 with right sides together; sew a ¼" seam with a small tight backstitch, sew three small stitches to finish.
Press seams open with an iron.
Repeat for the second square

Edging:
Straighten the grain of the edging fabric. Using the ruler, measure 3 ½" from the edge on the long side. Continue to measure and mark with the chalk in 3 places. Connect the dots by drawing a line with the chalk. Cut out the strip. Cut more strips as needed to finish the bag.

Lay the strip right sides together along the top of one square; mark the length of the top of the square. Trim the edging strip to the same length as the square. Sew a ¼" seam with a small tight backstitch, sew three small stitches to finish. Open the fabric out and press the seam open with your fingers. Repeat with the opposite side of the square.

Place a 3½" strip along the side of the 9-patch square ending at the outer edge of the bottom 3 ½" strip. Trim to match the square plus the edgings. Sew a ¼" seam with a small tight backstitch, sew three small stitches to finish. Open the fabric out and press the seam open with your fingers. Repeat on the opposite side.
Repeat for the second square.

Sides:
Using the ruler measure 3 ½" from the edge on the long side. Mark with the chalk in 3 places. Connect the dots by drawing a line with the chalk. Cut the strip out. Match the strip along 3 sides of one square to make sure it is long enough. If it is shorter, make another strip and sew it onto one narrow end of the 3 ½" strip.

With right sides together, place the strip along one side of the 9-patch block; sew to 1/2" from the bottom edge. Fold the strip at a 90* angle along the bottom edge of the square; make sure not to catch the fabric strip in the seam. Sew a ¼" seam along the bottom edge, sew to 1/2" from the opposite edge. Fold the strip at a 90* angle along the side edge of the square; make sure not to catch the fabric strip in the seam. Sew a ¼" seam along the side.

Add the Second Square in a similar fashion making sure to orient the Second Square similarly to the first. Lay the 9-patch square flat on a table and position the strips, right sides together, one strip at a time.

Lining:
Flatten the bag onto a table so that the strips bulge out at the sides. Measure from one side to the other. Multiply by 2 and add 1". This will be the length of the fabric for the lining. Measure from the top of the 9-patch square to the bottom of the flattened strip. Add 1". This will be the width of the fabric for the lining. Cut a piece of fabric with the length and width for the lining.

Fold the lining in half, short side to short side. Sew along 2 adjacent edges, with a 1/2" seam using backstitch; sew three small stitches to finish. Turn right side out. Turn the 9-patch bag inside out and place the right side out lining inside the bag. Sew along the top edge with a 1/2" seam using backstitch; leave a 2" space open. Turn the bag right side out through the space. Press the bag along the top seam tucking in the edges along the opening. Sew the opening closed.

Strap:
Cut out a 3½" strip from the fabric. Measure the strip over the shoulder to see if it is the right length, about 24". Cut a second strip the same size as the first strip. Place strips right sides together; sew a ¼" seam with a small tight backstitch along the long sides, sew three small stitches to finish. Turn right side out. Press with the iron. Tuck the ends inside the strap. Sew the strap onto the sides of the bag.

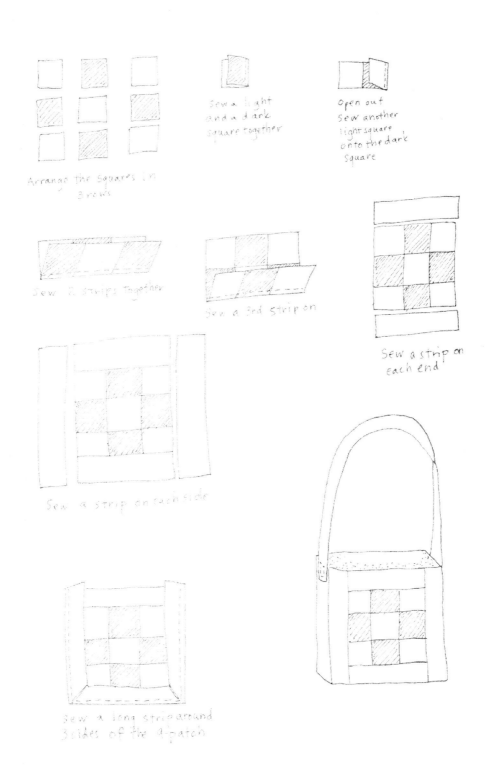

Arrange the squares in 3 rows

Sew a light and a dark square together

Open out Sew another light square onto the dark square

Sew 2 strips together

Sew a 3rd strip on

Sew a strip on each end

Sew a strip on each side

Sew a long strip around 3 sides of the 4-patch

Paper, 8 ½" x 11", several pieces
Pencil
Colored pencil
Scissors
Chalk
8 ½" x 11" Felt in Background color
Felt scraps
Embroidery floss
Embroidery needle

Design the Coat of Arms:
Draw a shield shape to fill most of the paper.

Divide the shield in half or fourths if desired.

Draw emblems on the shield. Designs can be found in books of coats of arms or online by looking up "coat of arms". Alternatively, use tools or symbols of a beloved craft, animal or activity, such as a sheep and spindle for a spinner. Color the design with colored pencils.

Cut the shield shape out.

Transfer the design to felt:
Place the shield shape on the felt background color. Trace around the edge with chalk. Cut the shield shape out of the felt.

If the shield was divided into halves or quarters, cut those shapes out of paper. Draw around the edges of the pattern onto felt scraps and cut out.

To create pattern pieces for the various designs on the shield: Lay a clean sheet of paper over the shield design or pieces. Trace the different shapes onto different parts of the paper so that each piece will be able to be cut out of the appropriate color.

Cut out the pieces needed to complete the shield design.

Lay the felt pieces onto the shield to form the design.

Sewing the shield:
Sew the lowest pieces onto the background shield first using the embroidery floss and needle. Blanket stitch or running stitch both work well depending on the situation.

Embroider small and/or narrow design elements with embroidery floss.

Paper-12" x 14" or big enough to stand on and fit both feet
Pencil
Scissors
Cardboard, cereal box or corrugated
¼ pound wool fleece
Washing Tub
Hot Water
Dish Soap
Ladle
Waterproof protection for tables
2 pieces of Bubble Wrap, big enough to cover the template about 12"x12"

Pattern and Template:
Stand on the paper with bare feet parallel and about 3" apart. Have a friend draw around your feet. Draw around the previous drawing about 1" away; connect the feet at the ankles. Cut out the pattern. Lay the pattern on the cardboard and trace around. Cut the template out. Or, alternatively, draw your feet directly onto the cardboard.

Wrapping the template:
Check the fleece to see how quickly it will felt: take a small piece of fleece, about the size of a dime; wet it with warm water and soap; roll between your palms gradually squeezing harder and harder, until the fleece has felted and the ball holds together. A quick felting fleece will felt in less than 5 minutes. If the ball does not form in 10 minutes of constant rolling, the fleece does not felt easily and it would be better to use a different fleece.

Stretch or pull the fleece into flat sheets. Wrap the fleece around the template: both feet and the ankle connection. Try to maintain a consistent direction. Wrap the template with more fleece going at a 90 degree angle to the first wrapping of fleece.

Fill the tub partially with hot water-as hot as is comfortable to touch. Add enough soap so that the water feels slippery. Lay the fleece wrapped template onto a piece of bubble wrap. Dip your hand in the hot water and sprinkle the water evenly over one side of the fleece wrapped template. Place the second piece of bubble wrap on top of the fleece. Pat the bubble wrap gently for several minutes. Flip the bubble wrap sandwich over. Lift the bubble wrap and sprinkle hot water over the second side of the fleece. Re-cover with bubble wrap and pat the bubble wrap gently for several minutes. Flip the bubble wrap sandwich over. Sprinkle hot water evenly over the first side of the fleece wrapped template. Continue patting and flipping until the fleece begins to hold together. Begin to press harder on the fleece and rub on the bubble wrap in a circular motion. It is easier if the bubble wrap is wet. Go over the edges of the template with a bubble wrap wrapped hand gently so as not to disturb the fleece but to begin to felt the edge.

When the fleece has begun to felt and holds together, test it by pinching a small section and lifting to see if it holds together. When fleece has felted, cut across the ankle between the 2 feet through the fleece and cardboard template. Flip the fleece inside out. Rub the boot between the bubble wrap to felt the outside of the boot.

Final felting can be done on the foot: slip the boot onto the foot and rub with the hands until the boot fits snugly. Repeat with other boot.

When the boot is fully felted, wash in running water until suds no longer run out.

Put the boots on to shape them. Remove them gently from your feet and set to dry. It may take several days for the felt to fully dry.

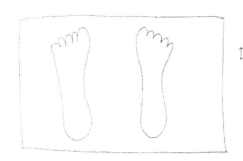

Draw around
the feet

Draw around
1"away from foot
Connect the feet
at the ankles

159

6th Grade Book

Elephant

Pencil Case

9-patch Bag

Felted Slippers

Felted Slippers

Opening

I stand in the light of my own being
And I recognize my power:
I am reason and nothing stands before my choice;
I am truth and so I live in the spirit
And so I live forever.

I am one with the whole:
What happens to the world,
Happens to me.

Closing

Steadfast I stand in the world.
With certainty I tread the path of life.
Love shall be in the depths of my being,
Hope shall be in all deeds,
Confidence I shall impress into my thinking.

Lesson Plan for Handwork

Grade seven:
THE GOALS FOR THIS YEAR ARE:
>   -To complete a doll with clothing
>   -To have the students take the initiative of interpreting instructions in their

handwork books so they can follow them
>   - To encourage students to help and learn from each other
>   -To stimulate the student to become aware of their own body and its spatial

relationships through the process of creating the doll and it's clothing
THE MAIN SKILLS TO BE INTRODUCED AND FURTHER DEVELOPED THIS YEAR
ARE:
>   -To introduce students to the process of watching a demonstration, taking

notes, then doing the step
>   -To learn to draw a pattern from instructions and proportions
>   -To learn to draw patterns from their own initiative
>   -To continue to build on previously introduced sewing skills
>   -To continue to learn to take the time to properly stuff and finish a project
>   -To understand the shape of clothing

TIME LINE OF PROJECTS: (Class is held 2 times a week for 50 minutes each)
>   August
>>   Handwork Book
>   September-March
>>   -Doll Head
>>   -Doll Core and Torso
>>   -Rose Windows
>>   -Doll Arms
>>   -Pattern for body
>>   -Sew body and legs
>>   -Attaching body and legs
>>   -Face
>>   -Hair
>   April
>>   -Doll Clothes
>   May-June
>>   -Beaded bracelet
>>   -Mystery Bag

The seventh grader is experiencing an awakening of the powers of thinking and protesting, as well as aesthetic capabilities. Appropriately, the seventh grade curriculum studies the artistic flourishing of the Renaissance and the rebellion of the reformation. It is important in teaching 12-14 year olds that the teacher gradually relinquishes authority, to work more as an equal with the students. This process comes from within the students. The teacher must remain watchful for the signs. The students are approaching physical maturity and becoming aware of body shape. As they mature emotionally, students are becoming aware of the many processes involving warmth: their own physical warmth; the warmth of affection and the fire of enthusiasm; a warm heart that glows like the sun and the light and warmth of other people. We continue to work with the three forces of head, heart and hands, but now they are transformed into intellect, heart-forces and will. Steiner said that of the three forces, the intellect is the most spiritual. However if developed in a one sided way, unsupported by feeling and will, the intellect develops a tendency toward materialistic thinking. By developing the will, through the dexterity of the hand, as we do in handwork, we lay a foundation for directing the intellect to the spirit. It is important for the seventh grade teacher to be prepared, both with tools and supplies as well as with a firm plan for the year.

Finished size 12" x 7 1/2"
      Cover: 1 piece of Cardstock- 12" x 15"
      Pages: 10 pages 11x 14" printer paper
      Tissue paper
      White glue
      Drinking straw
      Perle cotton or heavy thread/ weaving warp
      Chenille needle

Tissue paper cover:
Place the cover paper on a surface protected with newspaper or scrap paper. Spread glue evenly onto the cover paper. Tear tissue paper into irregular pieces about 3" x 4" in size. Pick up a piece of tissue paper using the straw by sucking the piece up with the straw and dropping it onto the cover. Press gently into place. Continue adding tissue paper onto the cover until it is mostly covered. Add more glue if necessary. Press all pieces flat. Glue can be added over the top of the tissue paper with a brush to secure all pieces. When you are satisfied with the design, allow the cover to dry.

Sewing the cover:
Fold the sheets of paper in half one at a time. Open out one sheet and layer one sheet on top of another sheet. Refold the paper as a group. Fold the cover in half and crease. Place the folded pages into the cover aligning the folds. Thread the needle with the Perle cotton or warp thread. Starting from the inside of the book, go through all the layers of the pages and the cover at the midpoint. Pull the thread through until a 4" tail remains. Go back through all layers ¼ of the way from the top edge; the thread is now inside the book. Go back to the outside of the book ¼ of the way from the bottom of the book; thread is now on the outside of the book. Sew back through the first hole at the midpoint. Arrange the thread tail on one side of the center thread and the needle and thread on the other side, tie a double knot. Trim the ends. The cover may be trimmed if it extends too far beyond the pages

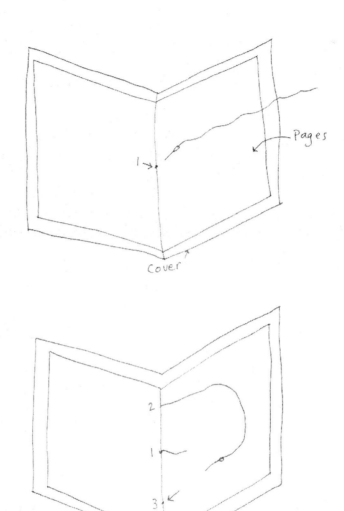

Pages

1 →

Cover

2

1

3

½ pound Wool Batting torn into 4" wide strips
Old sheets or fabric, torn into 2" wide strips, optional
1 ½" cotton knit tubing-18" long & -9" long
Cotton String- 36", 18", 60" & 12" long and some extra
Needles: general sewing needle, 2" Doll Needle and yarn needle
½ yard skin-colored cotton stockinette : 9" square for head; 19"x 6" for arms;
      approximately 10" x 14" for the body
Pencil or chalk
Thread: white, skin tone, red, basting and hair color
4" x 2" piece of red fabric, preferably silk
Dried Lavender
Shears and Scissors
Paper: 7" x 20" for arm pattern, 2 Pieces 8 1/2" x 11" paper taped together
      lengthwise for body pattern
Sewing Pins
Scrap Yarn in a light color for winding around arm and leg bones
Ruler
Embroidery Floss: eye and lip colors
Red beeswax crayon
Small, clean Rag
Tape Measure
Mohair yarn-straight or boucle in a hair color
Firm Cardboard or book
Crochet hook size J

The Doll Core

Group A:
Tear off 4-18" pieces of wool batting, (about as long as elbow to fingertip).
Layer 2 pieces to form a plus sign.
Layer 2 pieces to form a times sign or x.
Stack the x on top of the plus sign.

Group B:
Tear off 4-8" pieces of wool batting, (about as long as wrist to fingertip).
Layer 2 pieces to form a plus sign.
Layer 2 pieces to form a times sign or x.
Stack the x on top of the plus sign.

Place Group B on top of Group A.

Firmly wind a ball about the size of a golf ball from the old sheets or from more fleece.

Place the ball on top of the stacked fleece.

Pull the inside layers of fleece up around the ball gently, gradually adding the outer layers, until all the layers of fleece have been gathered around the ball to form a batting ghost.

Wrap twice around the fleece right under the ball with the cotton string and tie with a half hitch.

Hold the head up to see if the string is horizontal to ground level and adjust if necessary.

Tie very tightly.

Tubing

Prepare the tubing:
Connect the thread to the tubing with a knot ¼" from the top edge of the tubing. Sew a running stitch ¼" from the edge around the top of the tubing.
Pull the thread to gather together.
Knot the thread securely.
Turn right side out.

Doll Head:
Pull the tubing over the head firmly.
Wrap the 18"piece of string twice around the neck below the head.
Tie tightly.

Forming

Eye line:
Hold up the doll's head and find the face or the smoothest side.
Hold the string 12"from the end and place it where the right ear would be.
Holding the string at the right ear, wrap the long end of the string twice around the head ending at the right ear. Pull tightly to indent the fabric.
Knot to the 12" piece of string.
Check to see that the eye line is level and parallel to the neck string.

Chin:
Wrap the long end of the string over the top of the head and under the chin to form the cheeks; then bring the string back up to the right ear. Pull tightly to indent the fabric.
Knot firmly.

Ears:

With the needle and thread, make a knot at the right ear. Sew over the crossing of the strings at the right ear by making several long stitches forming an x. Knot the thread.

Preparing the tubing:

Sew a running stitch ¼" from the edge

Pull tightly to gather

Turn right side out.

Forming:

pull the tubing over the head.

Tie tightly.

Right Ear

2 wraps

wrap the long end of string around doll's head Pull tightly.

Tie firmly

12"

Wrap the long end of the string over the head and under the chin. Pull tightly and knot firmly.

right ear

stitch securely over the ears

slide

Slide the string down the back of the head

Repeat on the left side.

To form the skull, slide the eye line string down to the nape of the neck at the back of the head.

Skin

Measure around the circumference of the doll's head at the widest point. Cut out a piece of doll skin 9" x 9".

Lay the doll skin out flat, place the doll's head face down on the fabric with the grain running lengthwise. Pull the edges of the fabric tightly together around the doll head. Mark the overlap with a pencil.

Remove the doll's head from the fabric and fold in half lengthwise with edges matching. Draw a line along the edge at the pencil mark from the step above to designate the sewing line.

Sew along the sewing line with a tight back or running stitch; trim edges to ½". Turn right side out.

Pull the doll skin tube over the doll's head until only 1" extends past the top of the crown of the head. Adjust the seam to run down the back of the head, opposite of the face. Fold the 1" overlap fabric down neatly first on the right side; pin as needed to hold the fabric in place; stitch neatly in place. Fold fabric down neatly on the left side; pin as needed to hold fabric in place; stitch neatly in place. Fold the front flap of fabric towards the back; stitch neatly in place.

With the 12" piece of cotton string, tie tightly around the neck. Check to see if the neck string is parallel to the top of the head.

Check to see that the head seam runs down the back of the head, adjust as necessary.

Smooth any wrinkles to the back of the head.

Body Core

Prepare the tubing:
Knot the thread to the tubing ¼" from the top edge of the tubing. Sew a running stitch ¼" from the edge around the top of the tubing. Pull the thread to gather together. Knot the thread securely. Turn right side out.

Batting:
Lay a 16" piece of batting on a hard surface.
Lay a 14" piece of batting on top of the batting aligning one end with the first piece.
Lay a 12" piece of batting on top of the batting stack.

Roll up tightly beginning at the 4" edge and the thickest end.

Slide the rolled up batting into the prepared tubing. It should be slightly pear shaped.

Flatten the open end of the tubing and pull tightly around the batting. Tuck the fabric edges to the inside. Sew up the open end with the zipper stitch.

Heart

Fold 4" x 2" fabric in half lengthwise to make a 2" x 2" square.
With Needle and thread, using a running stitch, sew a heart shape on the fabric going through both layers. Leave a small opening.

Stuff with Lavender
Sew the heart the rest of the way.

Cut the heart out 1/8" - ¼" outside of the stitching.

Sew heart onto the upper left of the body core.

Adding the Body Core

Hold the doll head upside down.

Open out the layers of stuffing right down to the head core and neck string.

Place the top of the body core firmly against the neck string; make sure the heart faces the same direction as the face.

Pull the strips of head stuffing around the body core.

Pull the bottom edge of the head tubing over the fleece wrapped core.

Flatten out the lower edge of the head tubing side to side and tuck in the raw edges.

Stitch the lower edge together with zipper stitch.

Arms

Enlarge the Pattern by 10% or size appropriate to doll proportions.

Cut arm pattern out. Lay the arm pattern on a folded piece of paper so that flat edge is on the fold. Cut out

Fold the Doll skin in half lengthwise. Pin the fabric together in several places and baste around the 3 open sides.

Lay the arm pattern in the center of the fabric. Create the sewing line by tracing around the arm pattern with pencil or chalk.

With matching thread, sew a tight backstitch along the sewing line. Leave the middle space between the arms open.

Cut the arms out ¼" away from the sewing line all the way around as one unit. Make small snips around the curved areas on the hand. Snip between the thumb and hand being careful not to sever the seam.

Turn the arms right side out.

Arm Pattern

Leave Open

Don't Sew

Place on folded paper & cut out

173

Hands:
Wind a narrow strip of batting into a soft ball about the size of a walnut.

Slide the roving ball into the end of the arm to the hand.

Tie the wrist right above the stuffing.

Repeat for the other arm.

Arms:
Bones: Roll a 3" wide by 8" long piece of batting or roving into a tight cylinder.
Wrap the cylinder tightly with yarn until firm, leaving tufts of fleece at each end.

Cut off the tuft of fleece at one end of an arm bone.

Wrap the arm bone lightly with fleece and roll firmly between your palms, especially at the wrist.
Gather the skin back to the wrist on one arm and slip the trimmed end of the arm bone into place firmly against the wrist string.

Pull the arm skin up around the arm bone. The arm bone may need to be trimmed further. Wait until sewing the arms onto the body to judge further.
Repeat for the other arm.

Adding the Arms

With the thumbs pointing down, slide the open section between the arms over the doll's head.

The arm bones should fit comfortably on each side of the body core and be able to twist around so the thumbs point up. Are the arms the right length? Do the arm bones need to be trimmed to fit on each side of the body? If so, remove the arms and trim the arm bones as necessary. Replace the arms onto the doll.
Position the fabric between the arms close to the neck string.

Twist the arms so the thumbs point upward.

Stitch the arms into place along the edge of the fabric closest to the face and head using a whipstitch. Stitch the twist where the arms join the body into place.

Stretch the arm fabric out smoothly and stitch in place on the body around the bottom edge of the arm fabric.

Draw a 3" x 6" square in the upper left hand corner of the paper to record the calculations. Label it "Calculation Box".

1) Head length- from the neck-string to the top of the head: Hold the ruler parallel to the doll's head running up and down; align 0" with the neck-string and measure to the top of the head with the ruler. Write in the Calculation Box: "head length=_____".

2) Head width/Shoulder line- from side to side at the widest point: Hold the ruler parallel to the eye line at the widest point of the head; measure from side to side. Write the Calculation Box: "head width=_____."

3) Body length: divide the head length by 2; Add the answer to the head length. Write in the Calculation Box: "body length =_____."

4) Leg length –the same as the body length. Write in the Calculation Box: "leg length =_____."

5) Foot length- divide the head length by 2. Write in Calculation Box: "foot length =_____."

Making the Pattern

Draw a horizontal line 1" from the top of the paper; write your name on the right side of the paper.

Draw a perpendicular line 1" from the right edge of the paper

Shoulder line: beginning at the perpendicular line, mark off the measurement of the head width on the horizontal line. Drop a perpendicular line the horizontal line at this point.

Crotch line: Measuring down from the shoulder line, mark the body length on the parallel lines. Connect the marks to form the crotch line.

Leg line: Measuring down from the crotch line, mark the leg length on the parallel lines. Connect the marks to form the leg line.

Foot line: Measuring down from the leg line, mark the foot length on the parallel lines. Connect the marks to form the foot line.

Dividing the legs: Measure and mark the middle of the crotch line and the foot line. Connect the points with a line, call it the leg dividing line. Mark 1/16" out from the leg dividing line where it meets the crotch line. Mark 1/8" out from the leg dividing line where it meets the foot line. Connect the marks at the crotch line and the foot line. Mark 1/8" in from the outside edge of the perpendicular lines at the foot line. Connect the outer edge of the crotch line to the marks at the foot line.

Feet: Mark where the big toe would be with an "x" on each foot. Round the big toe edge of the foot. Draw a curve at the outside edge of the foot starting 1/2 way up the outside edge of the foot and ending 1/2 way across the foot.

Cut out the pattern starting at the top of the paper, include the 1" at the top; cut down the parallel lines to the crotch line; along the sloping lines of the legs and the curving edges of the foot and big toe; cut up between the legs to the crotch line.

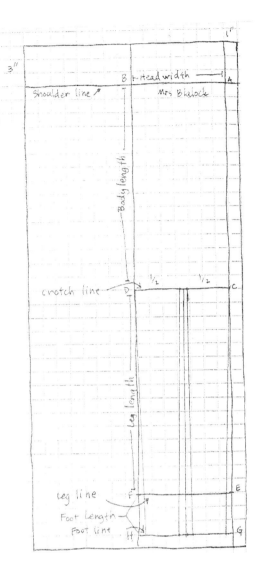

Body Pattern

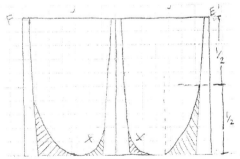

Detail of Foot
for Body Pattern

177

Fold the fabric in half with the grain running lengthwise.

Lay the pattern on the fabric with the grain running lengthwise.

Cut a rectangle out around the pattern leaving at least 1/2" of fabric beyond the pattern on all sides.

With contrasting thread, sew a running stitch around the edges of the fabric.

Lay the pattern on the fabric with at least ¼" all the way around.

Draw around the pattern with the pencil or chalk. This is the sewing line.

Sew on the sewing line using matching thread and a small, tight backstitch. Begin stitching below the shoulder line. Knot the thread securely.

Cut out the body and legs ¼" outside of the stitching.

Reinforce the crotch with a whipstitch in the seam allowance.

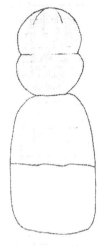

Head and Bodycore

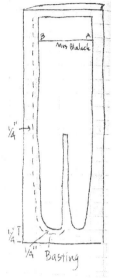

Leg and body fabric
ready to sew

whipstitch

Reinforce the crotch!

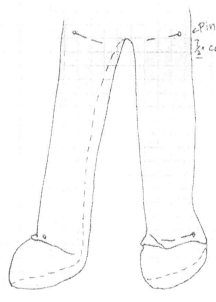

Pin
½" cut off leg bone

* Pin at hip joint

* It is better to err on th shortside when
cutting leg bones

* Dead space is necessary at the hip joint
for movement & mobility

Feet:

Roll a ball of fleece the size of a walnut.

Gather up the leg and place the fleece ball into the end of the leg.

Pack the fleece into the foot.

Pin the leg above the foot. Repeat with the other foot.

Legs:

Beginning at the narrow edge, roll a 4" by 12" piece of fleece into a tight cylinder.

Wrap the cylinder with yarn, pulling tightly.

Wrap the cylinder lightly with fleece; roll the cylinder between the hands to smooth and compact the surface.

Cut the excess fluff off one end of the cylinder to form the ankle.

Bunch the leg skin back to the foot. Press the ankle end of the cylinder against the foot fleece. Pull the leg skin up, holding the cylinder in place.

Pull the leg skin up around the leg stuffing. The top of the leg stuffing should end below the crotch. If it is longer than the crotch, cut off about ½" below the crotch. Pin at the hip joint above the leg stuffing.

Shoulders, Neck and Arms

Slide the doll head/core into the body. The side seams may need to be let out so that they stop under the arms.

Pull the shoulders up over the arms. If the fabric extends more than ½" above the neck string, trim the fabric to ½"above the neck string.

Flatten the front fabric flaps over the shoulders to the back. Pull the back flaps of the fabric over the shoulder, tucking under the edge so the fabric meets at the top of the shoulder. Stitch across both shoulders with zipper stitch.

Sew the body up to the armpits with zipper stitch.

Sew around the neck using zipper stitch. Catch and sew the fabric right above the neck string.

Tuck in the fabric around the arms.

Zipper stitch around the arm openings and down the arm seams if necessary.

lightly pad bumpy areas with wool

Adding the body core to the legs

Trim excess fabric

181

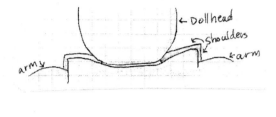

Pull shoulders up firmly

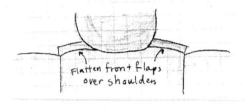

Smooth Front flaps to back Lap the back flaps forward

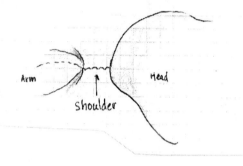

ZipperStitch together at Shoulder

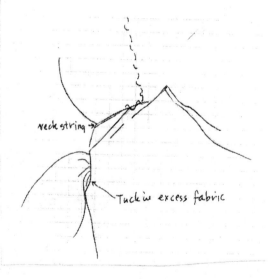

Tuck in excess fabric around arms and Zipper Stitch in place.

Fold the one foot up at a right angle and pin in place by pinning through the leg, foot and back through the leg.

Knot the thread at one side seam where the foot folds up. Zipper stitch the foot in place from side seam to side seam.

Define the ankle by sewing through the leg from one side to another. Pull to indent the leg slightly. Knot securely.

Repeat with the other foot.

Hip Joint

Unpin the legs below the body.

Knot the thread at the outside edge of the leg, right above the stuffing.

Sew through all the layers of the leg with a running stitch.

Sew at an angle, beginning higher at the outside edge of the leg, sloping down towards the inner leg. Continue stitching across the second leg.

Knot the thread and bury the end.

Belly Button

Mark the belly button with a pin on the doll's abdomen.

With a doubled thread, bury the thread coming out at the "holiest of holies"(also known as the crotch) between the legs. Secure the thread with 3 small stitches in the same place.

Push the needle and thread through the abdomen right next to the 3 small stitches coming out next to the belly button pin. Take a 1/8" stitch then return to the "holiest of holies." Pull the thread to dimple the stitch and create the belly button.

Repeat the above steps for 2-3 more stitches.

Make 3 small stitches where the thread comes out the last time. Hide the thread ends.

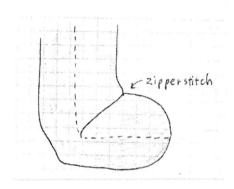

zipper stitch

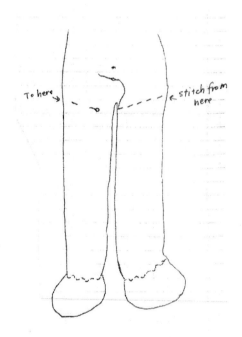

To here

stitch from here

* Mark the Belly button with a pin on the doll's abdomen

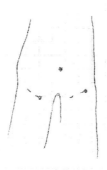

*in at A up
  to B

* In 1/8" away from B
  out at A

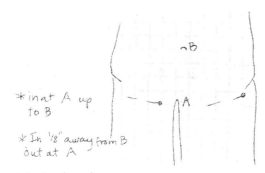

* Pull thread out at A, secure the thread with 3 small stitches - bury
  end of thread

Eyes

Mark the eyes and mouth with pins. The eye pins should be on the eye line string. The three pins should make an equilateral triangle.

Using eye color embroidery floss threaded into the doll needle, push the needle from the back or side of the head level with the eye line, under the future hairline, through to one side of a pin marking the eye placement. Leave a 4" tail to tie off at the end.

Sewing into the eye line, take a stitch slightly larger than ¼", returning just below the 1st stitch.

Take 2 more stitches; on the last stitch come out next to the second eye pin. Sewing into the eye line, take a stitch slightly larger than ¼", returning just below the 1st stitch.

Take 2 more stitches; on the last stitch go through to the back or side of the head coming out near where the thread went in.

 If possible tie the ends of the thread together.

Mouth

Mark each corner of the mouth with a pin. The mouth should be about as long as the space between the eyes.

Come from the back or side of the head with a doll needle with lip colored floss, leave a 4" tail and come out at one side of the mouth pin.

Stitch across to the other pin. Repeat the stitches 2-3 times. The second stitch can be slightly smaller than the first stitch.

On the last stitch, go through to the back or side of the head coming out near where the thread went in.

Tie the ends together, bury the ends under the hair.

Kiss of Life

Rub a red beeswax crayon onto a clean rag.

Rub the rag onto the doll's face at the cheeks.

The kiss of life needs to be redone periodically.

Long Hair:

Determine the finished hair length: with a tape measure, measure from the center top of the head to the desired length of the hair; double that length and add 2".

Find a book, a firm, piece of cardboard or something similar, that the yarn can be wrapped around to equal the desired length

Wrap the hair yarn around the form, either book or cardboard, 20 times.

Leaving the yarn on the form, sew along one edge with a backstitch and matching thread; cut the yarn along the opposite edge from the sewing.

Lay the hair on top of the doll's head and sew to the head along the hair's center seam line. Use matching thread and a sewing needle; sew the hair on with backstitch.

Sew around the hairline to secure the hair to the head.

Continue making layers of hair and sewing them to the doll's head to make the hair fuller.

Short hair:

With yarn and crochet hook, make a slipknot, chain 6, join to the first chain, loop formed.

Round 1: Work 6 single crochets into the center of the loop.

Round 2: Work 2 single crochets into each previous single crochet, 12 single crochets.

Round 3: *Work 2 single crochets into the first single crochet, work 1 single crochet into the next single crochet* repeat between *'s around; 18 single crochets.

Round 4: *Work 2 single crochets into the first single crochet, work 1 single crochet into each of the next 2 single crochets* repeat between *'s around; 24 single crochets.

Check to see if the disc matches the top of the doll's head. If it does, continue around working 1 single crochet into each previous single crochet until the cap fits onto the doll's head.

If the crown is too small, work another increase round: *Work 2 single crochets into the first single crochet, work 1 single crochet into each of the next 3 single crochets* repeat between *'s around; 30 single crochets.

Continue checking and increasing until the disc matches the top of the doll's head.

Continue working around making 1 single crochet into each previous single crochet until cap fits onto the doll's head.

Sew the cap to the doll's head.

Pattern
Fabric
Thread
Needle
Elastic-1/8"-1/4" elastic
Safety pin
Iron
Iron Board

Enlarge the pants pattern to the length from waist to foot, about 10" total length.

Fold the fabric in half. Place the pattern so the long straight edge aligns with the fold.

Make sure there is room to cut out a second pants section.

Pin pattern in place.

Cut out around the pattern.

Move the pattern to a new place along the fold.

Pin pattern in place.

Open out the fabric pieces. Place one leg onto the second leg, right sides together. Sew with a ¼" seam along one crotch seam. Repeat on the other side. Press open. With fabric inside out, fold the waist over ½"- press in place.

Stitch close to the edge of the fabric to create the elastic casing; leave a 1" opening to insert the elastic

Use the safety pin to thread the elastic through the casing.

Try the pants on the doll and adjust for fit.

Sew the ends of elastic together.

Sew up the opening in the elastic casing.

Hem the bottom edge of the pants legs: turn up the bottom edge of the pants leg 1/2"; press and sew in place

Align the crotch seams right sides together and flatten so the legs match up; sew the leg seams by stitching from one cuff, up the one leg, and down the other leg.

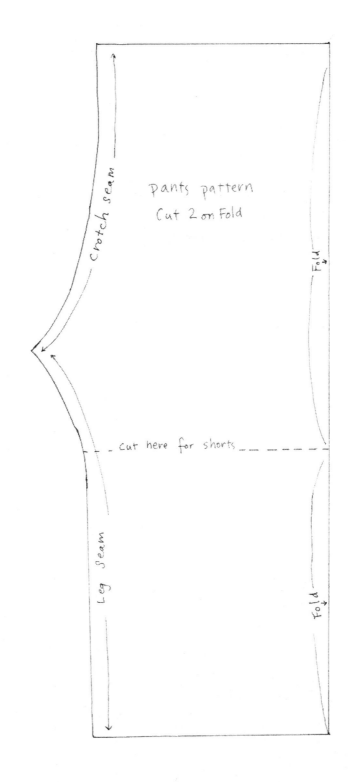

Pants pattern
Cut 2 on Fold

Crotch seam

Fold

cut here for shorts

Leg seam

Fold

190

Pattern
1/4 Yard Light cotton woven fabric
Thread
Sewing needles
Buttons
Snaps or Velcro

Before beginning, enlarge the shirt pattern to the same length as from neck to 1"
below doll's waist.

1) Fold fabric in half. Cut out 1 shirt back on the fold. Cut out 2 shirtfronts from the
edge of the fabric with the selvedge. Cut out 2 sleeves.

2) With right sides facing, sew one sleeve to each front at the arm edge

3) With right sides facing, sew the sleeves to the back at the arm edge

4) Hem the bottom edge of the front, back and sleeves

5) Turn under the neck edge ¼", press and sew in place

6) Fold the shirt in half along the middle of the sleeves so that the front side edges
match up to the backside edges, and the side edges of the sleeves match up. Stitch
from the cuff of the sleeve up the arm and down the side edges of the fronts and
backs. Repeat for the other side.

7) Sew buttonholes evenly spaced along the front edge. Sew buttons to match up to
the buttonholes along the opposite front edge. Alternatively, sew buttons evenly
spaced along the front edge and sew snaps or Velcro under the buttons to match up
to the buttons.

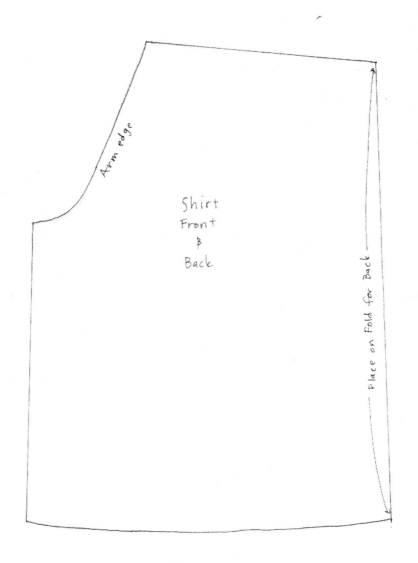

Arm edge

Shirt
Front
&
Back

Place on Fold for Back

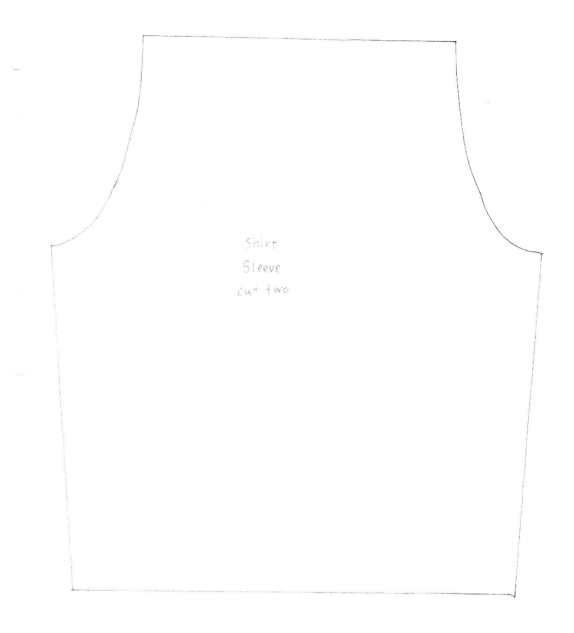

Shirt
Sleeve
cut two

11" x 14" paper
Ruler
Pencil
1/4 Yard cotton woven fabric
Thread
Sewing needles
Chalk
Bias Tape
Buttons
Snaps or Velcro

Sleeves:
Pattern:

1) With arms held out perpendicularly to the body, measure across the doll from wrist to wrist; add 1 ½". Draw a line on the paper the length of the wrist-to-wrist measurement.

2) Measure around the doll's arm at the widest point; add 1 ½". Starting at the line from step 1, measure and mark the arm width in 2 places. Draw a parallel line to the line in step 1.

3) Connect the ends of the lines in step 2 to create a rectangle.

4) Cut out the pattern; lay the pattern on the fabric; pin in place; cut out.

Sewing:

5) Finish the edges of the short sides of the sleeve fabric by turning the edges under ¼"; press in place; fold under another ¼"; press in place. Sew in place.

6) Measure around the doll body; divide in half and add 1 ½".

7) Measure across the sleeve fabric from step 5; subtract the sum in step 6; divide by 2. Measure from the center fold of the sleeve and mark the sum just figured with chalk.

8) Sew from the finished edge on one sleeve to the chalk mark; knot thread; repeat on the other side.

Jacket:

9) Measure around the doll's chest; add 1 ½".; measure from the doll's armpit to the desired length of the jacket. Cut a rectangle with these measurements.

10) Finish one long edge of the jacket fabric as in step 5.

11) Fold the sleeves in half so the wrists match; mark the fold with chalk; measure around the doll's neck; divide by 2= the neck opening; cut from the center fold, out along the top fold to create the neck opening; cut down the center fold on one side.

12) With right sides together, match the jacket piece to the sleeve piece. Sew with a 1/4" seam.

13) Finish the neck edge with the bias tape; slip the bias tape over the raw edge of the fabric; stitch in place.

14) Fold under the front opening edge ¼"; press in place; fold under another ¼"; press in place. Sew in place.

15) Sew buttonholes evenly spaced along front edge. Sew buttons to match up to the buttonholes along the opposite front edge. Alternatively, sew buttons evenly spaced along the front edge and sew snaps or Velcro under the buttons to match up to the buttons.

Dress:

16) Measure around the doll's chest; double the measurement for a slim skirt or triple it for a full skirt; measure from the doll's armpit to the desired length of the dress. Cut a rectangle with these measurements.

17) Finish one long edge of the dress fabric as in step 5.

18) Sew the short edges together with right sides facing using a 1/4" seam.

19) Fold the sleeves in half so the wrists match up; mark the fold with chalk; measure around the doll's neck; divide by 2 = the neck opening; cut from center fold, out along the top fold to create the neck opening.

20) With right sides together, match the dress piece to the sleeve piece. Sew together with a 1/4" seam.

21) Finish the neck edge with bias tape; slip the bias tape over the raw edge of the fabric; stitch in place.

Pattern-enlarge to ½" longer than the doll's foot
For slides: Rubber or foam material, such as old flip-flops
  1" Webbing
  Glue
For boots: felt or soft leather
Thread
Sewing needles

Slides:
  1) Cut 4 soles from the rubber or foam material
  2) Cut 2 pieces of webbing to go all the way around the foot
  3) Coat 1 side of sole material with glue
  4) Coat ends of webbing with glue
  5) Make a webbing sandwich: sole-webbing-sole
  6) Press together well. Set something heavy on top while the glue dries
  7) Repeat for the second slide

Boots:
  1) Cut 2 soles from felt or leather
  2) Cut 4 boot tops from felt or leather
  3) Sew 2 boot tops together along the front and back seams, wrong sides together.
  4) Sew boot top onto the sole
  5) Repeat for the second boot

Flats:
  1) Cut 2 soles from felt or leather
  2) Cut 4 flat tops from felt or leather
  3) Sew 2 flat tops together along the front and back seams, wrong sides together
  4) Sew flat top onto the sole
  5) Repeat for the second flat

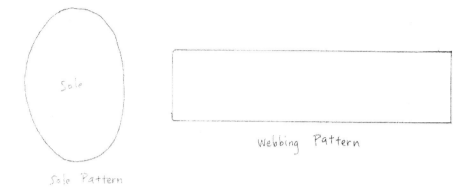

Sole Pattern

Webbing Pattern

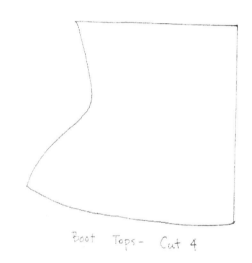

Boot Tops - Cut 4

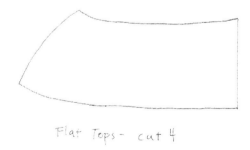

Flat Tops - cut 4

197

Graph paper
Colored pencils
1-5 ½" x 12 ½" x ¾" piece of wood
2- ½"x ½" x 5 ½" pieces of wood
Glue
Nails
Thin Crochet cotton thread
1" x 8" dowel
Beading needle
Nylon beading thread
Seed beads
Felt or Deerskin
Sewing needle
Thread
Button

If you want to create a design before you begin, draw a pattern on graph paper 7 squares by the length of the project.

Loom- Cut a 3/4" thick piece of pine 5 1/2" wide by 12 1/2" long

    Glue or nail a 1/2" x 1/2" x 5 1/2" piece of wood on the top at each end

Warp - Tape thin crochet cotton to the back of the loom and wind the cotton around the board lengthwise 8 times. Cut the cotton thread

    Un-tape the end of the cotton and tie the ends together tightly.

    Space the warp evenly in the center so each thread is about 1/8" apart.

    Slide a 1" x 8" dowel under the warp on the flat side of the loom.

Weave- 1) using a beading needle and the nylon thread, thread beads for the first row of the pattern onto the needle and slide to 6" from the end of the thread

    2) Pass the needle under the warp and press the beads up between the warp strands, 1 bead between every 2 threads

    4) Run the needle over the end warp and back through each bead; make sure the thread stays above the warp. Tie the end of the thread to the working thread

5) Thread the next row of 7 beads onto the needle

6) Pass the needle under the warp and press the beads up between the warp threads

7) Run the needle over the end warp and through each bead.

7) Repeat the last 3 steps until the design is finished.

8) Cut the warp threads in the middle of the un-beaded section and remove from the loom. Tie the warp ends together in twos or as a group.

9) Cut a piece of felt or deerskin the same width as the beading and as long as your wrist width plus 2"

10) Center the beading on the felt, tuck all warp thread ends and knots under the beading; Sew around the edges with a needle and matching thread

11) Sew a button at one end of the felt

12) Try on the bracelet and mark the bracelet for the buttonhole. Cut a small x into the end of the bracelet at the mark. Check to see if the button fits; adjust the opening if it is too small

13) Sew around the buttonhole with buttonhole stitch

Bead loom - side view

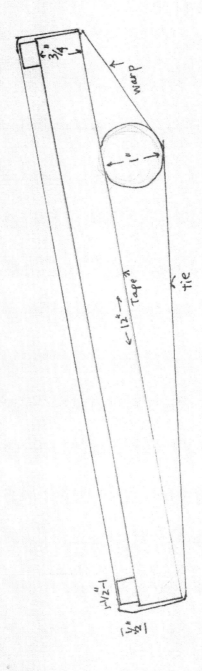

warp

3/4"

1"

12"

Tape

tie

1 1/2"

1/2"

To Weave:

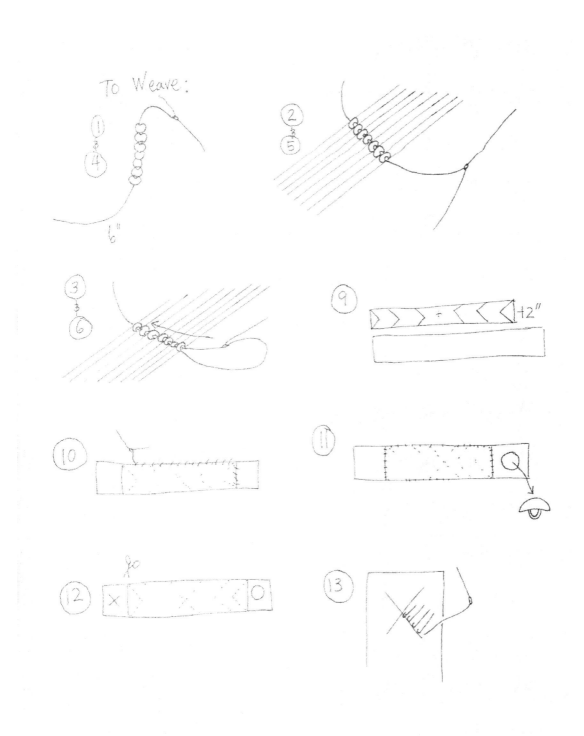

201

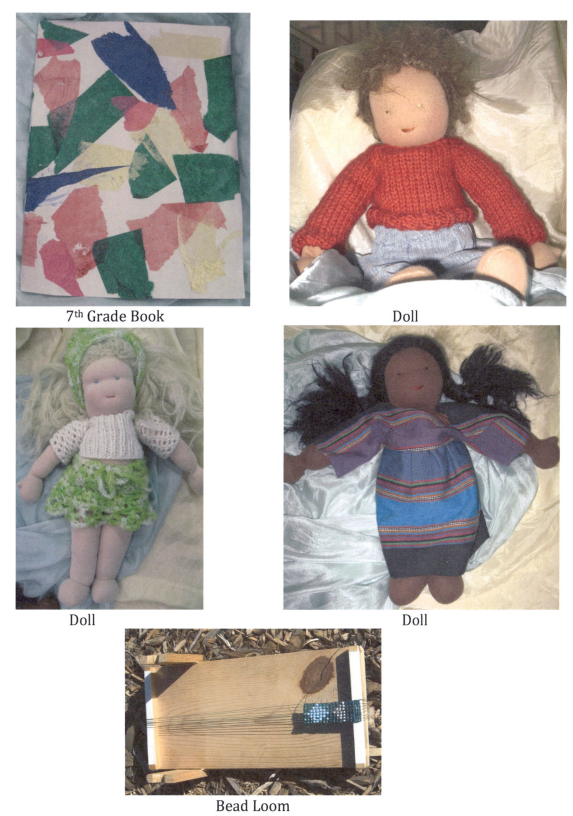

7th Grade Book

Doll

Doll

Doll

Bead Loom

Opening

Joy and woe are woven fine
A clothing for the soul divine,
Under every grief and pine,
Runs a joy with silken twine.

It is right it should be so,
Man was made for joy and woe,
When this we rightly know,
Through the world we safely go.

William Blake

Closing

Steadfast I stand in the world.
With certainty I tread the path of life.
Love shall be in the depths of my being,
Hope shall be in all deeds,
Confidence I shall impress into my thinking.

Lesson Plan for Handwork

Grade eight:
THE GOALS FOR THIS YEAR ARE:
- To foster a relationship with a machine
- To bring an understanding of the structure and function of sewing
- To bring an inner experience of cause and effect by making a pattern from their own measurements and sewing an article of clothing from it
- To further develop the understanding of what it is to be a human being
- To further develop the student's relationship to the world
- To engage the students' hearts as well as their minds
- To consider the practical value and significance for human life in the forces of the world
- To co-ordinate the foot pedal (will), hand skill (feeling), and attentiveness (thinking)
- To have an appreciation of all they have done in their eight years in handwork

THE MAIN SKILLS TO BE INTRODUCED AND FURTHER DEVELOPED THIS YEAR ARE:
- To learn to work with a machine including threading, sewing, and bobbins
- To have an understanding of fabric structure and grain
- To learn to work with precision
- To learn to take measurements and create a pattern
- To understand how to purchase fabric in a fabric store
- To keep a detailed account of the process
- To complete and turn work in on time

TIME LINE OF PROJECTS: (Class is held 2 times a week for 50 minutes each)
August
- Handwork Book
September
- Develop an understanding of woven fabric
- Definitions
- Machine drawing
- Naming parts on machine
- Straight of grain
October- November
- Handwork Bag
December
- Measurements for patterns
- PJ Pattern
January
- Trip to fabric store
- Seam allowances and cut out fabric
February-March
- Sew PJs

April-June

- Patchwork blocks
- Wallets
- Pillows
- Friendship Bracelets
- Second garment
- Patchwork blanket or pillow for their teacher

With puberty or "earth maturity," eighth grade students gain an inner experience for understanding cause and effect. Their very bones are coming to full length. They are experiencing resistance in their bodies. Since the awakening of the intellect in the seventh grade, they must be taught in clear-cut concepts. Students need to be given an understanding of human beings and the world they live in. We must engage their hearts as well as their minds. With the study of the advent of the industrial revolution, the students must consider the practical value and significance for human life in the forces of the world. Here is a quote that Alecia Dodge gave us for working with eighth graders:

"Love me most when I deserve it least, because that is when I really need it."

The eighth grade handwork curriculum begins by looking at fabric. Students are asked to look at fabric and answer the following questions: Which way was it oriented on the loom? Where is the lengthwise grain? Where is the widthwise grain? Do the threads intercross one after another or are some threads skipped to build strength or create pattern in the weave? They learn to find the straight of grain and why it is important to the lay of the final garment. When they go to the fabric store, they must discriminate between woven and knitted fabrics for their project. They begin to become aware of the fabric and weaving all around them.

Finished size 12" x 7 1/2"

> *Cover:* 1 piece of Cardstock- 12" x 15"
> *Pages:* 10 pages 11x 14" printer paper
> ½ cup Rice flour
> Saucepan
> Tempura or acrylic paint-purple
> Perle cotton or heavy thread/ weaving warp
> Chenille needle

Paste paper cover:

Mix ½ cup rice flour with ½ cup water. Stir until smooth. Bring 3 cups of water to a boil and pour into the rice flour. Stir constantly until thoroughly mixed. Add the paint a little bit at a time until the desired color is reached. Allow the paste to cool. Place cover paper on a surface protected with newspaper or scrap paper. Spread 2 tablespoons of paste evenly onto cover paper. Add more until paper surface is evenly covered. Use fingers, paint spatulas etc., to make designs on the cover. Designs can be reworked until a satisfactory design is achieved. When you are satisfied with the design, allow the cover to dry.

Sewing the cover:

Fold the sheets of paper in half one at a time. Open out and layer one on top of another. Refold the paper as a group. Fold the cover in half and crease. Lay the folded pages into the cover aligning the centerfolds. Thread the needle with 18" of Perle cotton or warp thread. Starting from the inside of the book, go through all layers of the pages and cover at the center. Pull the thread until a 4" tail remains. Go back through all layers ¼ of the way from the top, thread is now inside the book. Go back to the outside of the book ¼ of the way from the bottom of the book; the thread is now on the outside. Sew back through the first hole. Arrange the thread tail on one side of the center thread and the needle and thread on the other, tie the tail and needle ends of thread together, making a double knot. Trim the ends. The cover may be trimmed if it extends too far beyond the pages.

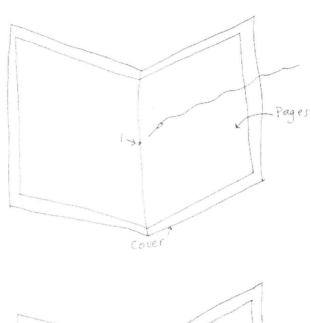

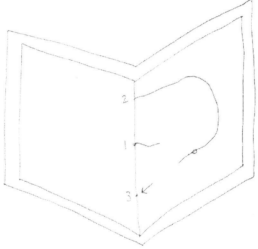

Cotton fabric-1/4 yard with selvedges

1) Warp - the first threads to be put on the loom
            -The stronger thread on the loom
            - Warp is the straight of grain
            - Warp is the lengthwise grain
2) Weft -the cross threads in a fabric
            -The weft is woven into the warp
            -The weft establishes the crosswise grain
            -Fabric pulled in the weft direction has more stretch than when pulled in the warp direction
3) Selvedge
            - The edge on either side of a woven fabric
            - The edge where the weft thread turns
            - Selvedges are usually denser than the body of the fabric
            - Selvedges run parallel to the warp threads
            - The selvedges are the least stretchy area of the fabric
4) Bias
            - Off of the straight of grain
5) True Bias
            -The bias when it is at a 45 degree angle to the straight of grain

Straight of Grain

Cotton fabric-1/4 yard with selvedges
Scissors

1) Hold the fabric up and establish the selvedges. Look for the cut edges.
2) Make a 1" cut at the selvedge edge ½"-1" from the cut edge of the fabric
3) Pick up a thread from the cut; pull the thread gently across the fabric. If the thread breaks go on to the next step.
4) Cut along the space made by the pulled thread. If the thread has broken, cut as far as the break, then pick the thread up and continue pulling. Once the thread has been pulled further, cut the fabric to that point.
5) The cut edge is the Straight of Grain.
6) The fabric will also rip along the straight of grain if pulled at the cut in step 2.

Have the students find the straight of grain on their piece of fabric.

Sewing machine
Handwork book or 8 ½" x 11" paper
Pencil

Make a very detailed drawing of the sewing machine from the front right, so that the hand wheel and the on/off switch are visible

The Sewing Machine

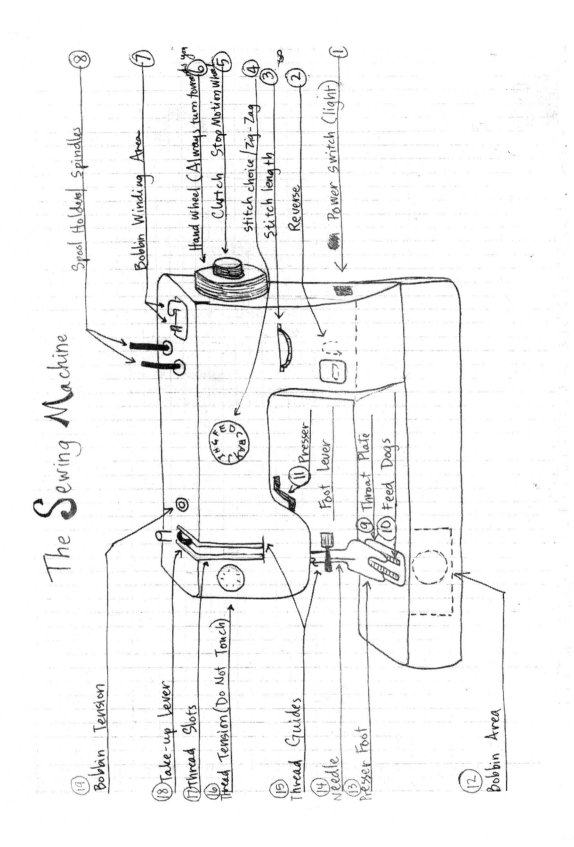

Spool Holders/ Spindles ⑧

Bobbin Winding Area ⑦

Hand wheel (Always turn forward to you) ⑥

Clutch Stop Motion Wheel ⑤

Stitch choice/ Zig-Zag ④

Stitch length ③

Reverse ②

Power Switch (light) ①

Bobbin Tension ⑲

Take-up Lever ⑱

Thread Slots ⑰

Thread Tension (Do Not Touch) ⑯

Thread Guides ⑮

Needle ⑭

Presser Foot ⑬

Bobbin Area ⑫

Presser Foot Lever ⑪

Throat Plate ⑨

Feed Dogs ⑩

Class 1:
Sewing Machine Drawing with names left off
Pencil
Chalkboard
Chalk
Sewing Machine

Put a drawing of a sewing machine up in the middle of the chalkboard.

Extend lines out from the different parts of the sewing machine. Number the lines.

Set a sewing machine in front of the class.

Go through the parts of the machine one by one and explain each part and its function.

Point it out on the machine as well as the drawing.

Help students locate the parts on their drawing if their machine is different from the one in the drawing.

Have students fill in the names of the parts of the machine as they are explained.

Class 2:
Next class, give the students a test on the names of the parts of the sewing machine by giving them a blank generic sewing machine drawing and having them fill in the names.

Give the test a second time to the students who miss more than 2 answers.

Make sure the students label all the parts on the drawing of the machine they will be using.

1) *How to put the machine away:*
   Foot Pedal: a) Wrap the cord around the pedal
   b) Place the pedal under the machine arm

2) *Sitting at the Sewing Machine:*
   a) Clear the Tabletop
   b) Place the foot pedal on the floor under your right foot with the low end forward
   c) Place the machine 1" from the edge of the table
   d) Sit directly in front of the needle
   e) The left foot is on the ground
   f) Sit forward in the chair
   g) Turn the hand wheel until the take up lever is at its highest point

3) *Sewing:*
   a) Place the material under the presser foot
   b) Lower the presser foot
   c) Place the left hand stretched out on the left side of the needle to steady and guide the fabric
   d) Turn the hand wheel with the right hand to make the first two stitches
   e) Press the foot pedal gently to begin sewing
   f) Sew to the end of the seam, removing any pins as you come to them

4) *Ending the seam:*
   a) Lift the foot from the foot pedal
   b) Turn the hand wheel until the needle is at its highest position
   c) Lift the presser foot
   d) Remove the material to the back
   e) Cut threads at least 2" long on the machine side

Sewing machine-unthreaded
Paper patterns-4-8 ½" x 11" pieces of paper printed with:
1) Straight lines-about 1" apart
2) A 6" square
3) A 6" square spiral
4) Two concentric circles; one 7" diameter; one 4 ½" diameter

1) Straight lines:
    a) Place the paper under the presser foot so that the line can be seen through the slot in the sewing machine foot
    b) Lower the presser foot
    c) Manually turn the hand wheel so that the needle enters and exits the paper twice; gently press on the foot pedal until the needle begins moving
    d) Sew to the end of the line-lift your foot off of the foot pedal
    e) Lift the presser foot; slide the paper off to the back
    f) Increase the stitch length; sew the next line
    g) Continue to sew the lines using different stitch lengths until all the lines have been sewn

2) Square:
    a) Place the paper under the presser foot so that the line can be seen through the slot in the sewing machine foot
    b) Lower the presser foot
    c) Manually turn the hand wheel so that the needle enters and exits the paper twice; gently press on the foot pedal until the needle begins moving
    d) Sew to ½" from the corner, lift your foot off of the foot pedal, turn the hand wheel by hand to the corner, end with the needle in the paper at the corner
    e) Lift the presser foot, turn the paper 90 degrees so that the next line is in line with the presser foot
    f) Continue around the square as in steps b-e

3) Square Spiral:
    a) Begin at the outside end of the line
    b) Work as for step 2 above, turning at the corners

4) Circle:
    a) Place the paper under the presser foot so that the line can be seen through the slot in the sewing machine foot
    b) Lower the presser foot
    c) Stitch slowly while turning the paper with both hands held flat on the paper, one on each side of the presser foot

5) Staple the pages into your handwork book.

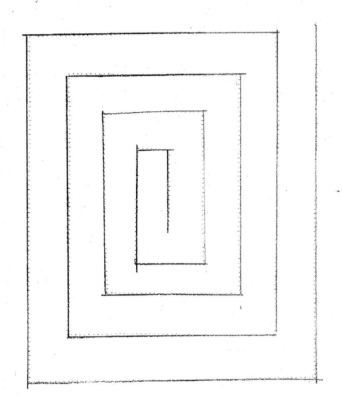

Sewing Machine
Spool of Thread

1) Place the spool of thread onto the spindle

2) Bring the thread around the thread guide

3) The thread goes down the thread slot and back up again around the back of the take up lever

4) Take the thread around the back of the take up lever and back down to the thread guide above the needle

5) Thread the needle from front to back

6) The thread goes between the toes of the presser foot to the back

7) The bobbin thread should be showing and taken to the back also

* Turn needle to highest position
* Spool on Spindle
* Thread Guides
* Take up lever
* Thread Slots
* Thread Guides
* Needle
* Pull to back of machine w/ Bobbin Thread

01

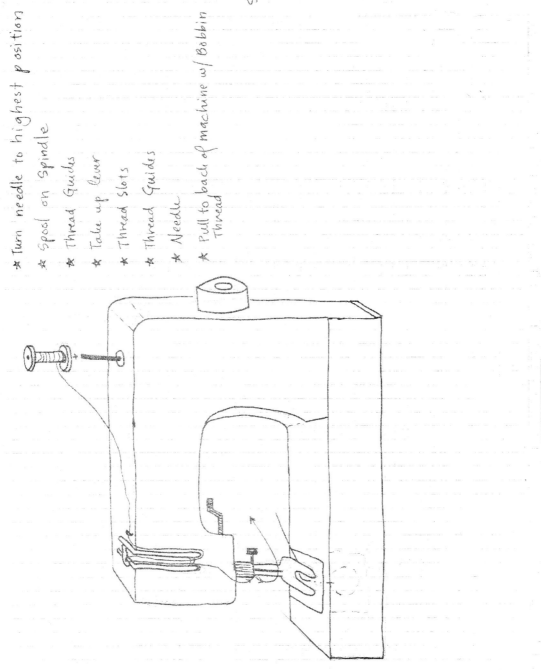

221

Sewing Machine
Cotton Fabric- 4"x6"-Several Pieces
Thread

1) Lay 2 pieces of the fabric together, matching the edges

2) Place the fabric under the presser foot so that the right edge of the fabric is on the 5/8" mark on the throat plate

3) Lower the presser foot

4) Turn the hand wheel with the right hand to make 3 stitches forward

5) Press the reverse button- make 3 stitches backwards

6) Begin pressing the foot pedal gently and continue to sew to ½" from the edge of the fabric; turn the hand wheel to the edge of the fabric

7) Press the reverse button-make 3 stitches backwards

8) Sew forwards to the edge of the fabric

9) Turn the needle to the highest point

10) Lift the presser foot

11) Remove the fabric to the back of the machine.

12) Cut the thread 2" from the needle

13) Press the seam open

Practice making both ¼" and ½" seams: follow the above steps placing the fabric at the appropriate mark in step 2.

2 pieces of 15"x 17" Cotton Fabric
Thread
Sewing Machine
Iron and Ironing board
Sewing pins
Ribbon- 1" wide, 1/3 of a yard
Cotton worsted weight yarn

Sewing together:

1) Lay one of the 15"x 17" pieces of fabric onto the other piece of fabric, right sides together, aligning sides and matching edges
2) Sew along one long side, turn the corner and sew across the bottom, turn the corner and sew the second side.
3) Fold the top edge under ½"; press in place
4) Fold the top edge under again 1 ¼"; Press and pin in place.
5) Sew around close to the edge of the first fold.
6) Turn the bag right side out

Finishing:

1) Cut the ribbon into 6- 1 ½" pieces.
2) Space the ribbon strips evenly around the top edge of the bag
3) Sew back and forth across the bottom and top edges of each ribbon strip
4) Finger knit a cord with the cotton yarn long enough to go all the way around the bag
5) Thread the finger knitted cord through the loops and tie the ends of the cord together

To take measurements:
1) Tie a string at the true waist
2) Pull the measuring tape until it is snug
3) Make sure the measuring tape is level to the floor

PJ Measurements   *Ease*
1) Waist measurement – measure around the   =_____
   waist at the string
2) Hip Circumference- around the fullest part   =_____+4"=_____
   of the hip
3) Hipline-from the waist to the fullest part   =_____
   of the hip
4) Crotch Line-the side measurement from   =_____+2"=_____
   the waist to the seat of the chair
   a) Sit in an armless chair
   b) Measure from the waist string to the chair seat
5) Out seam – from the waist string to the floor =_____
6) Divide the Hip + Ease by 4   =_____

IV) Pattern:
1) Hip (#6 above)   _____
2) Hipline (#3 above)   _____
3) Crotch ((#4 above)   _____
4) Out seam ((#5 above)   _____

Paper for pattern-newsprint or paper on a roll cut to 48" long by 36" wide
Pencil
Yardstick

Note: All measurements will be from part IV on the Measurements for Pj's worksheet

1) Fold the paper in half lengthwise; open paper out; using the yardstick, draw a line down the centerfold.

2) Draw a line 3" from one end of the paper perpendicular to the center fold- Mark this line the "waistline".

3) Mark the intersection of the two lines "A"

4) Point B-Measure down from point A along the center line the length of the out seam; make a dot.

5) Draw a line at point B perpendicular to the centerline -mark this the "hemline"

6) Point C-At the Waistline, measure from Point A to the left the length of the Hip measurement; mark it point C

7) Point D-At the Waistline, measure from Point A to the right the length of the Hip measurement; mark it point D

8) Point E-Measure down the center line from A the length of the Crotch line; mark it point E.

9) Draw a line perpendicular to line AB at point E; -mark this the "crotch line."

10) Point F- Measure to the left along the crotch line from point E the length of the Hip measurement; mark it point F

11) Point G- Measure to the right along the crotch line from point E the length of the Hip measurement; mark it point G

12) Connect points C and F; Label the line *"front"*

13) Connect points D and G; Label the line *"back"*

14) Point H- add ½ Hip measurement + ¼ Hip measurement

_____ + _____= a_____

Divide by 2 = a_____ divided by 2 = _____
Measure out from point F on the crotch line and mark Point H
Measure out from point G on the crotch line and mark Point I

15) Point J – mark ½" in towards the center on line AD
    Measure up 1" from the mark just made- mark point J
    Draw a line from A to J

16) Point K- Measure and mark ½" in from point C towards point A; label it point K

17) With a curve draw a line from point J to I on the *"back"* line

18) With a curve draw a line from point K to H on the *"front"* line

19) Measure out away from the center along line FH 1 ½" from F. Mark point L.

20) Measure out away from the center along line GH 1 ½" from G. Mark point M.

21) Measure around your ankle and heel. Add 2". Divide by 2
    Heel+2"=_____divided by 2 =_____ankle length

22) Measure from point B to the left, the ankle length; mark it point N.

23) Measure from point B to the right, the ankle length + ½"; mark it point O

24) Draw a line from L to N.

25) Draw a line from M to O.

26) Point P- Measure down 6" from L on line LN; label it P.

27) Using the curve connect H to P.

28) Point Q- Measure down 6" on from M on line MO; label it Q

29) Using the curve connect I to Q.

30) Measure from point B ½" to the right. Mark it point R.

31) Draw a line from A to R.

32) Cut out from A-J-I-Q-O-R-A. Label it "Back"

33) Cut out from A-K-H-P-N-B-A. Label it "Front"

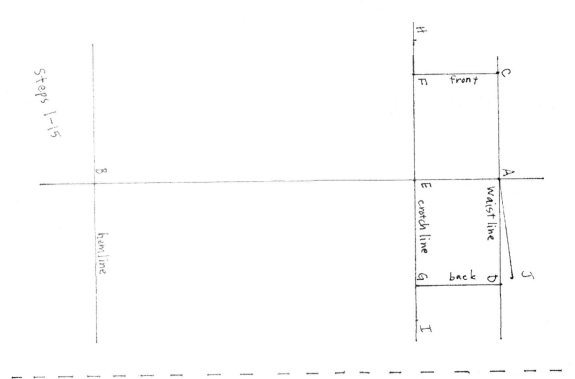

Steps 1-15

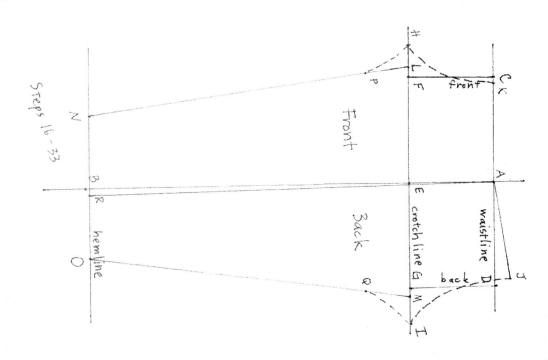

Steps 16-33

227

Determining the Yardage

Paper-21"wide by 90" long
Pattern pieces
Tape measure

1) Lay the paper out on a flat surface such as a table or the floor.

2) Lay the pattern pieces side by side with the waists at opposite ends

3) Slide the leg pattern pieces towards each other until they no longer fit on the paper. The pattern pieces should be ½" from the edge of the paper and at least 1" between each other to allow for seam allowances.

4) Measure from waistband to waistband; add 3" for waistband seam allowance

5) Divide the measurement by 36" to figure the number of yards of fabric needed for the PJs.

Visiting the Fabric Store

It has become a tradition to ride to the fabric store on the bus, get our fabric, then go for a walk to the beach, bring our lunch and ride back to school on the bus. It is great for the students to go through the process of actually picking out, requesting the yardage and purchasing their fabric. I highly recommend going to the fabric store with them. The class before the trip, I have them write down these guidelines.

1) Remember! We are representing the school and all future students of the school. Appropriate behavior is expected at all times.
2) Find the fabric from the agreed upon areas of the store. Fabric is to be woven, not knit and 100 percent cotton.
3) Check the bolt end for the width, fabric content and price per yard.
4) Check with the teacher regarding the appropriateness of the fabric.
5) Carry the bolt to the cutting table.
6) Politely tell the salesperson the yardage required
7) Watch the fabric being cut
8) Carry the fabric and the paper tag to the checkout counter and pay for the fabric
9) Take the fabric home. Wash and dry it as you normally wash and dry your clothes.
10) Bring it back to our next class

Materials
2 ½ yards of 45" wide woven cotton fabric, either flannel or plain
Iron and ironing board
Pattern
Pins
Tailors chalk
Clear ruler
Shears
Sewing Machine
Thread
1 yard - ¾" elastic
Large safety pin
Hand sewing Needle

Seam Allowance and Cutting Out the Pattern

1) Press the fabric

2) Straighten the grain at one end of the fabric

3) Check to see if the fabric grain is straight by folding the fabric in half lengthwise. If the edges and corners match up without causing wrinkling, the fabric is okay. If wrinkles run across the fabric when folded in half lengthwise or if cut ends and selvedges do not line up when the fabric is folded, have two people hold the fabric one at each cut end and pull gently to straighten the grain.

4) Fold the fabric in half lengthwise and lay on a tabletop or the floor.

5) Lay the pattern on the fabric so that both pieces are ½" away from the edge of the fabric and there is at least 1" of space between pattern pieces.

6) Pin the corners of the pattern so they lie smoothly on the fabric

7) Add pins every 4"-5" along the pattern

8) With tailors chalk and a ruler, add ½" seam allowance on the sides of the patterns and 1 ½" at the waist and hems.

9) Have the teacher check the pattern lay out and seam allowance

10) Cut the PJs out on the seam allowance. Leave the patterns pinned to the fabric

1) With chalk label the fabric pattern pieces *"front"* and *"back"*

2) With right sides together, pin one front to one back along the inseam from the crotch to the hem. Leave the curve from the crotch to the waistline unpinned.

Note: the front and back pattern pieces will not match up on the out seam side. That is okay. They are different sizes on purpose.

3) Sew from the crotch to the hem with a ½" seam

4) Press the seam open and flat

5) Repeat with the other front and back

Crotch seam

1) With right sides together, match up one pant front/back with the other pant front/back.

2) Pin in place along the crotch seam

2) Sew a ½" seam along the crotch sewing line

4) Sew again 3/8" away from the edge of the fabric

5) Trim the seam allowances to ½ their width with shears

6) Press the seam flat

Out seams

1) Flip the pants so that a front out seam edge is next to a back out seam edge with right sides together. The new orientation should present an inside out front and back with two long legs.

2) Align the side seams: a front with a back on each side

3) Pin

4) Sew a ½" seam down each out seam

5) Press seam open

Elastic Casing

1) Fold over ¼" at the raw edge at the waistline of the pants. Press in place with the iron

2) Fold over another 1 ¼". Press in place with the iron

3) Pin in place, matching the side and front seams

4) Baste on the fold line from step 1 above, 1" down from the waistline

5) Sew close to the fold, leaving a 1" opening for the elastic

Elastic

1) To determine the elastic length subtract 5" from the waist measurement

2) Pin the safety pin to one end of the elastic

3) Thread the elastic through the casing at the waistline of the pants

4) Once the elastic is all the way around the pants, pin the elastic in place and try the pants on. If the elastic is too loose, adjust to the right fit. If the elastic is too tight, cut a longer piece and rethread it through the casing.

5) Overlap the two ends of the elastic by 1"; check for twists in the elastic; sew the elastic together with a square.

6) Sew up the 1" opening in the pants waistline invisibly by hand.

Hem

1) Try pants on.

2) Stand on a chair

3) Have a friend fold the pant leg under at the appropriate length; pin in place

4) Remove the pants

5) Turn the pants inside out; fold the leg fabric up all around to the same length as the pinned area; press in place.

6) Trim pant leg to 1 " past the fold. Fold the raw edge under ¼" and press in place.

7) Fold the hem into place; pin.

8) Baste close to the second fold from step 6.

9) Sew close to the fold.

10) Remove the basting

11) Trim all threads.

12) Congratulations!

2-hole, 4-hole, & shanked button
4" x 6" cotton fabric, folded lengthwise
Needle
Thread
2 toothpicks or small pieces of cardboard

Buttons are sewn on ½" from the folded edge of the fabric
 Always use doubled thread

1) *4-hole button*
   a) Thread the needle with 36" of thread, pull the ends together and knot the thread. Slide the needle between the layers of fabric and come up where the button is to be sewn on.

   b) Take 3 small stitches where the button is to be sewn on ending on the right side of the fabric.

   c) Go up through one buttonhole and down through another.

   d) Go through the fabric to the wrong side of the fabric.

   e) Slide a toothpick or small piece of cardboard under the sides of the button to create a space for the shank.

   f) Come back up through one of the previously used buttonholes and back down through another hole. Repeat using the same holes 3 times.

   g) Repeat steps c-f using the two remaining holes.

   h) Come up through the first hole and down the second hole but not through the fabric

   i) Make a ½ hitch between the fabric and the button around the thread to strengthen the shank; repeat 3 times.

   j) Sew through to the back of the fabric; make 3 small stitches and sew the end of the thread through the layers of fabric; trim thread close to where it exits the fabric.

2) *2-hole button*
   a) Follow steps a-f and h-j above

3) *Shanked button*
   a) Secure thread as in steps a-b

   b) Sew through the shank and back to the fabric 3 times

   c) Secure thread as in step j above

Handwork Bag

PJ's

Materials:

      4-6 pairs of #8 knitting needles
      worsted weight yarn: one ball in each of 4-6 colors
      Prizes-Balls of Rainbow Yarn
      4-6 chairs
      Chalk or rope to mark the starting point

1) Divide the class into teams with equal numbers of students. Give each team a name based on their yarn color.

2) The game can be played either inside or outside

3) Draw a line with the chalk on the pavement outside or carpet inside, or stretch a rope out for the starting line.

4) Have the students line up in their groups on the starting line.

5) Put the chairs a short distance away from the starting line. Cast on 15 stitches for each team. Place the knitting needles and yarn on the chairs.

6) Count down for the first students to begin.

7) The first student in each group runs to the chair, begins working, and knits a row. The student lays the work down on the chair and runs back to the waiting team.

8) The first student must tag the second student before they can start running down to the knitting. Failure to wait will result in a 10 second penalty.

9) Students continue to run to the chair, knit a row, and run back.

10) The first team to be back to the starting-line, wins the prize. Quality could also be taken into consideration.

11). Alternatively, when class time is down to the last 15 minutes make a loud sound, ring a bell, blow a horn etc. That signals the last row to be knit. The team with the most rows wins.

12) If the class is imbalanced or there is a student who is particularly knitting challenged, they can act as an official. They will need to keep an eye on the students to make sure they are really knitting, etc...

Brooking-Payne, Kim. Games Children Play. Gloucestershire: Hawthorn Press, 1996

Brown, Rachel. The Weaving, Spinning And Dying Book. New York: Alfred A Knopf, 1997

Dendel, Esther Warner. The Basic Book Of Fingerweaving. New York: Simon and Schuster, 1974

Glockler, Michael; Langhamner, Stefan; Wiechart, Christoff. Education-Health for Life. Dornach: Paramount Print Pack Ltd, 2006

Gosse, Bonnie; Allerton, Jill. A First Book of Knitting for Children. Gloucestershire: Wynstones Press, 1995

Grigaff, Anne-Dorthe. Knitted Animals. Gloucestershire: Hawthorn Press, 2005

Hauck, Hedwig. Handwork and Handicrafts. London: Rudolf Steiner Press, 1968

Johnson, Anne Akers. Hemp Bracelets. Palo Alto, California: Klutz Press 1998

Martin, Michael. Educating Through Arts and Crafts. Crawley Down: Steiner Schools Fellowship Publications, 1999

Meyebroker. Rose Windows. Edinburgh: Floris Books, 1994

Mitchell, David and Livingston, Patricia. Will-developed Intelligence. Fair Oaks, California: The Association of Waldorf Schools of North America, 1999

Rawson, Martyn and Richter, Tobias. The Educational Tasks And Content Of The Steiner Waldorf Curriculum. Great Britain: Fellowship Publications, 2005

Schneider, Michael S. A Beginner's Guide To Constructing The Universe. New York: Harper Collins Publishers, 1994

Sealey, Maricristin. Kinder Dolls. Gloucestershire: Hawthorn Press, 2001

Shaw, George Russell. Knots, Useful And Ornamental. New York: Bonanza Books, 1933

Spock, Marjorie. Teaching As A Lively Art. United States: Anthroposophic Press, 2006

Stockmeyer, Karl. Rudolf Steiner's Curriculum for Waldorf Schools. Stoarbridge: The Robinswood Press, 1991

Wilson, Frank R. The Hand. New York: Vintage Books, 1998

Sources

Dyes, Roving and Silk Fabric:
Dharma Trading Company: Petaluma, CA (800) 542-5227
www.**dharmatrading**.com/

Fleece:
West Earl Woolen Mill: 110 Cocalico Creek Rd, Ephrata Township, PA 17522
(717) 859-2241 **westearlwoolenmill**.com/

Hemp Fabric:
Eco Vigor Fabrics: 33476 Alvarado Niles Road, Suite 7, Union City, CA 945873188
(510) 487-8199 ecovigor@sbcglobal.net

Knitting Needle Blanks:
Twin Birch Products: 117 E 2nd St, Siler City, NC 27344
(919) 545-0098 www.**twinbirchproducts**.com

Notions, Cross Stitch Fabric, Perle Cotton and craft supplies:
http://www.waldorfsupplies.com

Yarn:
Brown Sheep Yarn: 100662 County Road 16, Mitchell, NE 69357
(308) 635-2198 **brownsheep**.com/
Lamb's Pride Worsted, Burly Spun and Cotton Fines Worsted